AF425659

"In a world filled with distractions, Veldhuizen reminds us of God's desire to draw the church into the overarching story of the Bible, focusing on those who are 'far off' from the gospel. Far Off Saints cuts through the noise, conveying God's heart for the lost."

Mark Batterson, NYT bestselling author of The Circle Maker

"This is not a God-forsaken world--quite the opposite. God so loved this world that He sent His Son so that whoever believes in Him might not perish but have eternal life. Far Off Saints is a calling to the Church to rediscover and return to her noble calling to take the Good News of Jesus Christ to those who have yet to hear--near or far. It's a calling to slumbering Christians to reawaken and reignite the Pentecost fire that defined and drove the Early Church in supernatural power, come what may. It's a calling to reconnect with our divine mandate and eternal purpose and the relatable teaching style of Ivan Veldhuizen reminds us to draw close to a God who first drew close to us so that we might draw others unto Him."

Reverend Dr. Lisa Pak, Partners & Networks (Asia) for Finishing the Task & Kingdom Impact Network (KIN) Catalyst for Wycliffe USA

"There are many good things vying for the attention of the church. In Far Off Saints, Ivan Veldhuizen reminds us that God has a heart to pull the church into the grand narrative of the Bible, prioritizing those who are "far off" from embracing the gospel message. Concise, clear, and motivating, this book is designed to break through the distractions and communicate God's heart for the lost."

Ted Esler, PhD, President, Missio Nexus

"I come across people all the time who are longing for a greater sense of purpose and significance. With scriptural teaching and real-life stories, Far Off Saints lifts our sights, moves our hearts, and helps every believer see that they really have a valuable part to play in God's global mission. I am so excited to bring this practical tool to my congregation!"

Rev. Mark Albrecht, NorthBridge Church, Antioch, IL

"God's people are given God's Word not as a mantle piece but as a training manual with marching orders. Far Off Saints is a comprehensive action plan to catalyze movement toward the greatest cause of all: The fulfillment of the Revelation Promise. It should come with a warning: Don't begin this journey unless you wish to see your world and yourself transformed."

Rev. Gregg Heinsch, Lead Pastor, Celebration Community Church, FL

"I have had the honor and privilege of knowing Ivan Veldhuizen for over 15 years and the joy and delight of working with him recently. His commitment to the gospel of Jesus Christ, his insights in the word and his encouragement in this study will motivate you and encourage you in your walk with Christ. I encourage you to read and embrace this book and I am sure you will be empowered to run your race till the end."

Dr. John K Jenkins Sr., President Converge
Pastor, First Baptist, Glen Arden, MD

"Through compelling stories, eye-opening facts, and deft Scripture analysis, Ivan Veldhuizen's book, Far Off Saints, will challenge all who read it to reflect carefully and prayerfully on God's mission in this world, and our involvement in it. Useful as a supplement for daily devotions, or by small groups and Sunday School classes, Far Off Saints will bring you up to speed with what God is doing both near and far. I highly recommend this book!"

Larry W. Caldwell, Academic Dean, Kairos University
Senior Missiologist, Converge

"Far Off Saints is a powerful four-week experience that will launch you and your church into wonderful new arenas of global impact! The videos and supplemental materials are so good."

Steve Richardson, President, Pioneers USA

"Followers of Jesus may be too preoccupied to be obedient to his commands. The church may have veered off course from its intended purpose. However, 'God is a missionary God,' and he has not failed in his purpose. Through many stories, you will see that God is at work, yet there is more work to be done. God has designed us and his Church to have a role in his plan. Far Off Saints stirs us to realign our hearts and our churches with God's plan for us: 'Go and make disciples of all nations.' It may not be easy, but it will be worth it. Whether you are a new follower, a seasoned pastor, or a veteran missionary, get ready to be moved and challenged to be part of what God is doing around the world.

Deb Mashburn, Project Leader

Serving in West Africa with Converge International Ministries

"Far Off Saints is a deeply compelling and spiritually stirring work that challenges readers to reimagine their role in God's mission to reach the unreached. The vivid stories, from the remote Himalayan mountains to the icy tundra of Siberia, beautifully illustrate the power of the gospel to transform lives, even in the most forgotten corners of the world."

Brian Weber, Converge MidAtlantic

Regional President & Executive Minister

Far Off Saints

*Remembering the Revelation Promise
and Your Place In It*

Ivan Veldhuizen

Arrival

This book is dedicated to all those men and women who are investing their lives to bring the gospel of Jesus to those who are far off. Your dedication, perseverance and sacrifice inspire me and fuel me to be the best version of Jesus' disciple that I can be, for His glory.

Contents

An Invitation to Draw Near

The apostle Peter was on fire! The Holy Spirit had powerfully infused the man as he stood before the perplexed masses of people at Pentecost. With godly conviction, he unashamedly declared,

*Repent and be baptized every one of you in the name of Jesus Christ for the forgiveness of your sins, and you will receive the gift of the Holy Spirit. For the promise is for you and for your children and **for all who are far off**, everyone whom the Lord our God calls to Himself! Acts 2:38-39*

Peter got it. It took him three years of living in the shadow of Jesus, but he finally got it. This Kingdom of God—this new life, miraculous regeneration, gift of the Holy Spirit—was for all people near and far. When the Holy Spirit gripped him, he understood Jesus' intended design for the first time. He realized he could do nothing else but be all in on God's plan for the human race, for those near and those far off.

When I think of far off saints, I'm transported to the towering peaks of the Himalayan Mountains in Sikkim, India. A few friends and I traveled nearly ten hours through some of the most remote regions of this majestic mountain range on treacherous roads with falling rocks. On a couple of occasions, all of us needed to exit the vehicle and walk quite a distance because the mountain roads were washed out by recent downpours. If our vehicle failed to make it across, it would plummet thousands of feet to the forested abyss below. While experiencing some seriously intense moments, we had lots of laughs along the way too. My friend, David Nelms, founder of The Timothy Initiative, still swears he saw a monkey reading a newspaper along the road as we drove by!

Our goal was to visit the first believers in this hard-to-reach region of the world. A small house church had started through a woman who came to know Jesus in another part of India. She returned to her people to live, and bring the gospel to her family and friends who had never heard of Jesus.

Our entourage was five hours late because of the treacherous condition of the roads. When the mountain road ended, we still had a quarter mile hike along the precipice of the mountain ledges to find the home where the church awaited. As we approached the rugged shanty, a person greeted us in his native language, a gaping smile on his face. The group of new Himalayan believers had been huddled together for hours waiting patiently for us to arrive.

It's difficult for me to describe what happened there that night. Reflecting back on it now, it truly seems surreal—almost like a dream. We had a brief conversation with the group of 30 through an interpreter. The church planting leader was giddy as she profusely thanked us for coming all this way to visit and see what God was doing among them. But here's what I remember the most. They sang. It was only two songs in their heart language, but even without understanding a word, the Spirit of God gripped us all. It was powerful! Though far off, remote, simple, uneducated, and unsophisticated, this church experience was probably the most powerful connection with God I had ever experienced.

When the two songs were finished, we asked if they would sing one more song—we were so moved by their worship. Immediately, there arose a somewhat hushed but animated conversation among the church members. It went on for what seemed like a full minute. We Americans were a little surprised that such a simple request would bring so much chatter among them. And then the interpreter looked at us and stated, "We are very sorry. We have only written two worship songs so far. We do not have another that we can sing."

Here, among these far off saints, worship songs were being written because they had none from anywhere else. Among these remote believers, a church was being developed that was completely fresh and emerging out of their culture, history, traditions, and biblical understandings. It was beautiful.

There are people groups and segments of populations all around the world where future far off saints await. With no gospel presence, no disciples currently exist, no church has been established, and no missionaries have been sent. Though far off to us, they are near to the heart of God. Long ago, Jesus came for people just like this. As Peter stated at Pentecost, "This promise is for you, your children and for all who are far off."

There is something else that we may need to recognize as being far off. Us. Yes—those of us who have been redeemed by the blood of Christ. His saints. We may be far off—Far Off Saints. Could it be that we have overlooked, never embraced, or forgotten the critical calling that Jesus gave to all his followers? God has commissioned his church to "disciples the nations." There is no plan "B".

Fallacies have permeated the church, especially here in America:

» "We can't really do much to bring the gospel to people groups still unreached in the world."

» "The days of the western missionary are over."

» "We need to focus on where we are. There's plenty to do here."

Let me challenge you in these four weeks of engaging with Far Off Saints. Would you open your mind and heart to receive fresh things that God might say to you and your church? That's all I ask. Choose to be sincerely receptive. Ask God to open your spiritual ears, soften your heart, release any stymying grip on your current orientations and see what new thing God has for you.

Jesus gave us a glimpse of what's ahead. The vision was given to John in Revelation 7:9-10:

After this I looked, and behold, a great multitude that no one could number, from every nation, from all tribes and peoples and languages, standing before the throne and before the Lamb, clothed in white robes, with palm branches in their hands and crying out with a loud voice, 'Salvation belongs to our God who sits on the throne, and to the Lamb!

This is the revelation promise. Every people group in the world will be represented before God in this majestic worship gathering at the end of time as we know it. Not one segment of humanity will be missing. This is God's promise. And this is our commission as God's saints.

And he came and preached peace to you who were far off and peace to those who were near. For through him we both have access in one Spirit to the Father. Ephesians 2:17-18.

My hope and prayer is that in these days of contemplating God's Word, reflecting on God's heart, and dialoguing with God's people, you will be stirred in new ways with God's plan for his people. I pray that all will be brought near—far off saints here and far.

Ivan Veldhuizen

"Let me challenge you in these four weeks of engaging with Far Off Saints. Would you open your mind and heart to receive fresh things that God might say to you and your church? That's all I ask."

How To Get the Most Out of This Study

Far Off Saints is a multi-faceted study, designed to inspire and challenge you in numerous ways. To get the most out of these four weeks focusing on missions, here are a few suggestions.

1   Take a few minutes each day—five days a week—to read, contemplate, and respond to the book you hold. As you are immersed in the Word, let it wash over you and stir your heart.

2   Gather or engage with a small group using the small group guides included. Online video teaching and Biblical discovery will provide opportunities to dialogue and process important concepts with others.

3   If this is an all-church experience with Sunday teaching as well, be sure to participate each weekend, taking notes in the sections provided. Good things happen when the entire church commits to pursue this as one.

4   Pray a lot. Simply open your mind and heart for what God may want to say to you in these important days.

Who Are the Far Off Saints?

The world is filled with people who do not know God, but represent a segment of the population we'll call far off saints. It's an already but not yet term for lost people. They are not redeemed, but should be, can be and some will be. God desires that all are saved and come to a knowledge of the truth. If we're honest, most of these people are not on our minds much, but they are always on God's mind! Many live with the greatest injustice in the world—to be born, live and die and never hear of Jesus. God is at work among these far off saints in new and fresh ways. Some are far away by distance, culture, religion and social standing; and many live right among us, but are still far from God. There are complex challenges to reaching these individuals and peoples with the good news of Jesus. And that's why we will dig deeper, understand more, acquire God's heart for the lost, and see if we can be vital participants in bringing these far off saints into the family of God.

PENTECOST IN SIBERIA

"What am I doing here?!" My brain was pounding the question as I navigated the Aeroflot steps onto the windblown tarmac of Vorkuta, Russia. It was 20 degrees below zero with a stiff wind that drove the freeze-factor down even more.

I grew up in rural America. My world was simple and mono-ethnic. I heard about missionaries as I grew up, and was fascinated by the stories of risk and adventure from those who went to far off places in order to bring the gospel. But that seemed like a different world to me. Maybe I should have cared more, but it was far removed and didn't register with my heart much. Still, as I developed spiritually and searched the Word of God in my college and seminary years, I realized I was missing something about God's plan for the world and my part in it.

In March of 1993, I was asked by the Billy Graham Association to be the lone representative and site technician of a first-ever satellite crusade in this tundra city of 200,000. Communism had recently fallen. The tiny surviving church there was still skittish about going public.

This was my first ever mission trip. It was cross-cultural in every way. Vorkuta was previously a political prisoner site for Stalin—he sent thousands of people there who opposed his policies. These political prisoners worked in the numerous coal mines that surrounded the city. People generally lasted 6 to 12 months before they died of black lung disease, a result of working in the two-mile depths of the coal caverns without any protection. Though this happened a generation earlier, the offspring of these people were profoundly shaped by the dark days of Stalin and the years of oppressive communism that followed. Numerous times I heard the Russians state that "the railroad tracks are built on the bones of dead men." They claimed you could hear their remains creak as the trains lumbered by.

It was in this environment of oppression and depression, burdened with a dark and morbid history, that I had the rare opportunity to see the gospel publicly proclaimed to thousands who had no hope. We had rented the largest venue in the city, a hockey arena that held 3,000 people. The local believers worked hard to prepare. A priority for them was mobilizing prayer, asking the Lord by name to bring lost people to know Him.

I had thought what happened at Pentecost, with 3,000 souls being saved, was a thing of the past. But when the invitation was given that first night, I saw something I never imagined I would see—half the crowd ran to the front of the venue and fell on their faces. Many were weeping, others ecstatic, some somber as they committed their lives to Jesus Christ. On that first night, over 1,500 decisions were made. This happened two more nights as the three-day crusade continued. At the time, this response rate was the highest of any crusade Billy Graham had ever held—over 52% of those who attended made a decision to follow Jesus!

Something happened to me during those days in that cold, despondent, oppressive city as I witnessed God transforming lives in the midst of the cruel conditions these people faced. I saw God working in this far off place in the world in ways that blew my mind. I knew that for the rest of my life I needed to be deeply engaged in bringing the gospel to the lost peoples of the world–here, near and far.

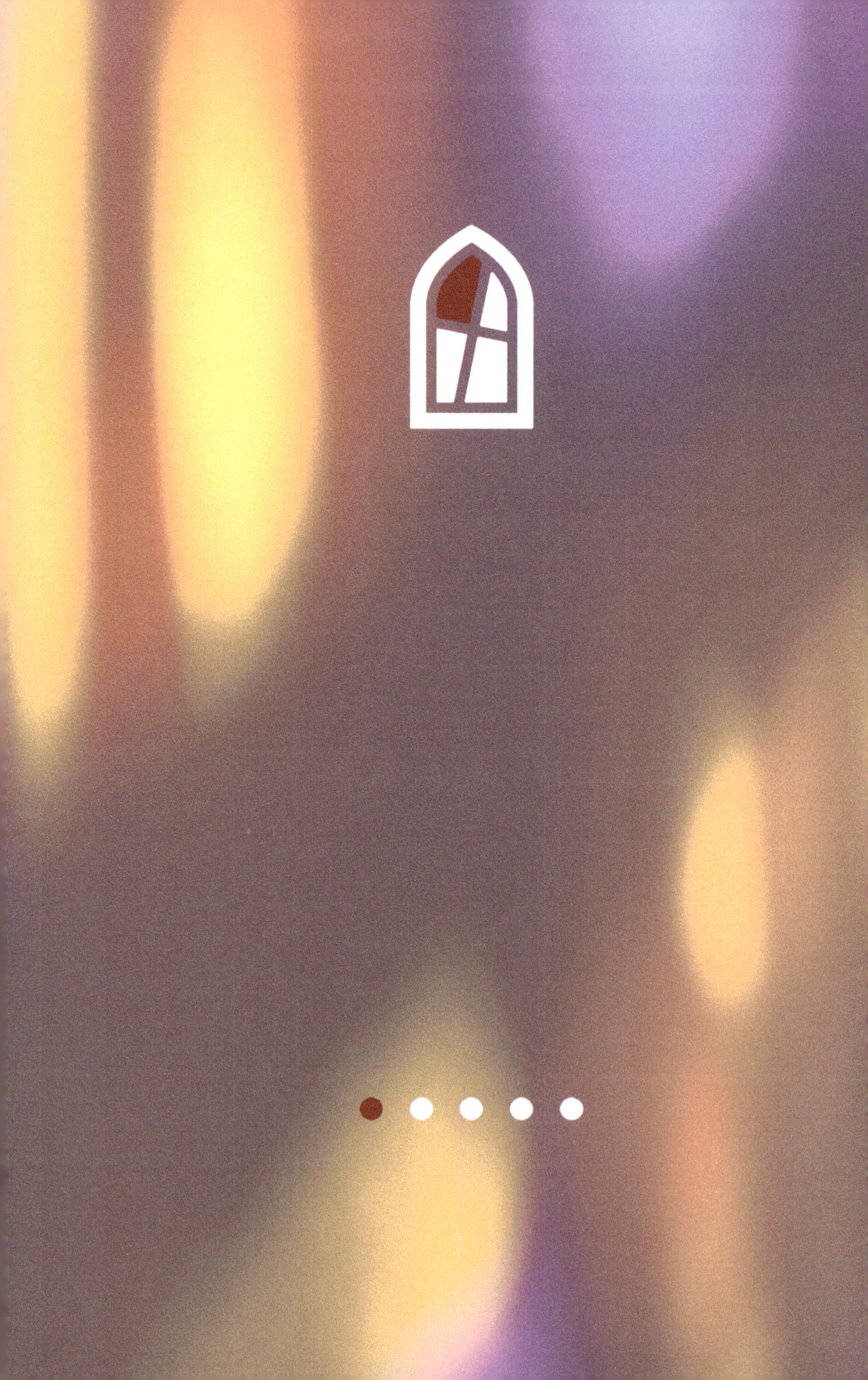

God Constantly Pursues Far Off Saints

Could it be that God's highest priority in the world is to bring the gospel to all peoples? And if so, should that affect our priorities as his followers and Church?

We can easily become the center of our own universe. Christians and churches can often slide into the "Jesus is here to give me happiness" fallacy. We can convince people to follow Jesus because he will provide for all of their needs or give them what they're looking for. The truth is, our happiness and fulfillment are not God's ultimate objective. Yes, he cares for us a lot, but his plan is much bigger than our self-serving desires and agendas.

Consider God's word for the Apostle Paul upon his conversion: "I will show him how much he must suffer for my sake." That doesn't sound like a step in the right direction if Paul wanted a nice easy life! No, Jesus was calling him to engage in a great cause—God's plan for the world.

GOD LOVES FAR OFF SAINTS

A rare opportunity was given to me in 1993 when I visited Vorkuta, Russia. On one particular day, I was escorted to some tundra dwellers outside the city—Nenet people living on the snow and ice, fending off nature to survive. These people lived in huts made of caribou skin, wore caribou leather for their clothing, cooked over open fires and lived a day-to-day existence without any knowledge of Jesus. Few people have ever noticed this remote tribe, but God has had his eye on them from the beginning. He is determined they will not be overlooked or forgotten, because our God is driven for every ethne' (people group) in the world. His heart beats for these far off saints. He calls our hearts to be shaped in the same way.

Jesus pronounced an enlightening statement in Matthew 24:14, "This gospel of the Kingdom shall be preached in the whole world as a testimony to all nations, and then the end will come."

The disciples wanted to know when Jesus' Kingdom would be established and when he would take his place on the throne. By his answer, Jesus clarified the determination of God for all mankind: every nation will have an opportunity to hear, know and follow Jesus before the end comes. This reveals God's passionate pursuit of all people groups in the world, so much so that he will suspend the culmination of all things until the gospel has penetrated every corner of the earth.

This determination to complete the evangelization of all nations, people groups, ethnicities, and segments of every society on earth is not a peripheral goal in God's mind and heart. It is central. In fact, all God does and all that he will do is driven by this commitment to see this happen. He already gave his son to provide salvation for all mankind. He will also be sure that all the world is exposed to the truth of God's love for them.

GOD IS DRIVEN TO FINISH THE TASK

This complete evangelization of the world will not happen by chance. God is driving his agenda, inviting us to be critical participants here, near and far.

In the Scripture passage addressed today from Matthew 24, notice the completeness of realities to come—"whole world" and "all nations". Again, in Psalm 86 we see the expression, "all the nations." Not one people-group is

> The word for "nations" in Matthew 24:14 is the Greek word *ethne*, meaning people groups or ethnic groups. It is not referring to geopolitical nations.
>
> The word for "nations" in Psalm 86:9 is from the Hebrew word *goy*, most often referring to a specific people group or nation, often in reference to gentile (non-Israelite) peoples.
>
> The words of the Psalmist will someday finally be fulfilled:
>
> "All the nations you have made shall come and worship before you, O Lord, and shall glorify your name." Psalm 86:9

overlooked. Every single one matters to God. There are large people groups still unreached, like the six million Wolof in West Africa, and there are small people groups that are lost, like the 6,100 Aralles of West Sulawesi, Indonesia. Every single one matters to God and should matter to us. God has brilliantly included us as his disciples into his plan to get this task done.

The mission I lead recently sent out a team of five to find an overlooked people group in Mauritius, a small island nation between Madagascar and Australia. We heard of a large Deaf population there who have never had any known believers among them. The Deaf are cut off from almost every culture in which they exist, needing to create their own *ethne* amongst themselves. This is how they survive and make a life out of what they have. Our team was there for a week and, by God's providence, found inroads to the Deaf of Mauritius.

Meredith Henderson, a member of the team, describes what happened:

During our week in Mauritius, we spent time with Deaf people from all over the island. As we expected, when it comes to Sign Language, we found Mauritian Sign Language to be different from American Sign Language. There was enough similarity that with some effort and by God's grace, we could effectively communicate. Sadly, what we soon learned was that the

Deaf there lacked an understanding of who God is. To our knowledge, there were no followers of Jesus in the Mauritian Deaf community.

On our first full day, we met with the leadership of an NGO that provides job placement training for Deaf people. While there, we met Christopher & Suffian, along with other Deaf adults. We were led to spend more time with Christopher and Suffian in the days ahead, spending several hours with them at times. Two of our teammates had the opportunity to clearly explain the Gospel to Christopher in sign language. He responded and asked to be baptized. At the end of the week, after hearing the Gospel as Christopher shared his salvation story, another young Deaf man, Yeshdev, came to saving faith and asked to be baptized the next day.

This is so exciting! These are possibly the first Deaf believers ever in Mauritius! Hopefully, it is only the beginning of a very great harvest there. Our Deaf Catalyst Team continues to meet via Zoom with these new believers in Mauritius through a Discovery Bible Study. This continues to fuel the passion they have to share the good news of Jesus to other Deaf in their island nation. Many seeds have already been planted. We eagerly anticipate a great harvest of Deaf believers in Mauritius and then a movement to fan out to the neighboring countries across the Indian Ocean.

"This determination to complete the evangelization of all nations, people groups, ethnicities, and segments of every society on earth is not a peripheral goal in God's mind and heart. It is central."

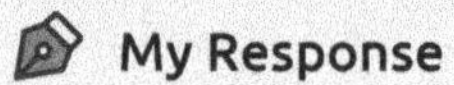 My Response

PERSONAL REFLECTION:

Which Scripture passage today challenged you most and why?

OBSERVATION:

Of the stories you read today, along with the Introduction, which do you wish you could have been a part of and why?

Learn more about all those people who are still waiting to receive the gospel

I've put together a variety resources to help you learn more about the many unreached people groups around the world.

faroffsaints.com/god-pursues

ACTION STEPS:

Is there anything God is prompting you to do or address right now? Jot that down in the space provided.

So Many Far Off Saints

The greatest injustice in the world is to be born, live and die and never hear of Jesus.

Oswald J. Smith, a Canadian pastor and missionary advocate in the 1900s, stated, "We talk of the Second Coming; half the world has never heard of the first." Though this was a fact 50 years ago, it is still true today. The world has massive cultural, geographical, social and religious pockets completely devoid of anything Jesus. The best assessments tell us that 29% of the world's people have no access to the gospel at all. At the time of this writing, this represents three billion people. Among these peoples, there are no believers, no churches, and no Christian witness in any form. If someone in those people groups even knew enough to ask about Jesus, there is no one there to tell them or disciple them into a relationship with God. 70,000 die every day among these people groups without ever having an opportunity to hear about Jesus! That's one person who will die every 1.23 seconds.

I have so many questions and feelings as I ponder these facts:

» Has the church failed in its task of global discipleship?

» What kind of awakening will it take for the church to finish the task given at the Great Commission?

» Is the church even aware and concerned about the state of the world without Jesus?

» Am I doing my part in this, or should I do more?

And he made from one man every nation of mankind to live on all the face of the earth, having determined allotted periods and the boundaries of their dwelling place, that they should seek God, and perhaps feel their way toward him and find him. Acts 17:26-27

By the Numbers *(approximate)*

17,000 People groups in the world

7,000 Unreached People Groups (UPG's) in the world

1,300 Unengaged Unreached People Groups (UUPG's) in the world

29% The segment of the world's population that has no access to the gospel. They have no known believers, no Bibles, no gospel radio, no printed materials and no church exists in proximity to them.

THE MAGNITUDE OF THOSE FAR OFF

I love the above verses. In light of the overwhelming facts we began with today, this Scripture reminds us of the sovereignty and capability of God. The Apostle Paul delivered these words to a crowd completely unaware of our Creator God. While they were worshiping the Unknown God in Athens, Paul encouraged the crowd to keep looking for the truth about the God that can be known. Within this Bible passage, there is also an undeniable statement about God arranging the affairs of mankind so that his purposes will be accomplished. He has "determined allotted periods and boundaries…that they should seek God…and find him." The task before us is too much if we take God out of the equation. But when God is factored in, the possibilities are much different. We must also realize that his followers and his Church cannot be taken out of the equation. The magnitude of the task will only be accomplished by God's supernatural power and the Church's determined obedience to Jesus' directive.

THE CHALLENGE OF REACHING THOSE FAR OFF

Missions has been the most complex thing I've ever been a part of. The barriers confronted in reaching a people group are staggering—language, culture, religion, misinformation, deeply seated mindsets and traditions, political influences, family dynamics, spiritual strongholds and much more. Short-term missions do have a role but will never accomplish the task of "discipling all the ethne" of the world. For most of the people groups still unreached, it will take years of persistent commitment, sacrifice, unwavering engagement, creative strategies, God-given wisdom and Holy Spirit fire to make inroads to the hearts and minds of those blinded by the darkness.

Again, Acts 17 reminds us that God has a plan! He is not ignorant of the challenges before us. He lacks nothing in fervor or commitment to see these lost people come to know him. He has "determined allotted periods and boundaries" for all the peoples of the earth to know him eventually. It remains paramount that we, his people and his Church, are attuned to his promptings, ready to follow wherever he leads and whatever the cost.

THE FAR OFF WHO ARE INSULATED AMONG US

Did you know that the United States claims the fourth most unreached people groups of any nation on earth? We truly are a melting pot with people arriving from all cultures and religions of the world to embrace the American Dream and enjoy the freedoms we share. In this unique era in history, with travel being easier and more accessible than ever, God is moving people across the face of the earth, many to our cities and neighborhoods. This is called the diaspora, Greek for "scattering" or "dispersion." For many people groups, it has been challenging for us to go there, but God is bringing them here so that they might "perhaps feel their way toward him and find him." They may be feeling their way toward him right across your street or in the cubicle next to you at work.

Don't miss this important element, however. These new Americans are naturally insulated from the gospel right among us.

We have neighbors from Sri Lanka living across the street from us. Though they have been in the U.S. for decades, they have never had any exposure to the Christian faith nor the truth about Jesus. When Mina (not her real name) heard of our home church and our open invitation to come, she asked if she could attend. We were delighted when she started showing up! She had never held a Bible in her hands, heard of the gospel and had no idea what salvation meant. She loved the warmth of our group and the practical ways we were living our faith in the community around us. After a three-hour lunch conversation with my wife, Susan, she is more aware than ever how her Buddhist beliefs drastically contrast with ours. It will be a long journey for her to find her way to God, but we are now walking that journey with her.

How can the diaspora right among us be so far off where the gospel is completely available?

» People live primarily within their own cultures. Just as we don't generally seek information on Hinduism or Shintoism, they won't independently seek information on Christianity.

» These unreached peoples will rarely, if ever, attend our churches—it's too much of a cultural, psychological and emotional hurdle.

» Authentic relationship is how the gospel is transferred. We Americans rarely cross our comfortable social parameters to reach out to others very different from ourselves.

» Very few believers are walking across the street to meet these new Americans on our turf in a way that will effectively engage them in a journey toward Jesus.

Yes, the Apostle Paul declared God's handiwork beautifully when he stated,

And he made from one man every nation of mankind to live on all the face of the earth, having determined allotted periods and the boundaries of their dwelling place, that they should seek God, and perhaps feel their way toward him and find him. Acts 17:26-27a.

Like a blind person feeling their way in an unfamiliar place, a helping hand or a little guidance goes a long way to help. That's our part in God's big plan to see far off saints come to faith in Jesus.

PERSONAL REFLECTION:

Jot down three words describing how you feel after reading about the complexity and size of the task that remains for global evangelization?

OBSERVATION:

What people groups are living right around you that may be insulated from the gospel? Try to name at least three.

Learn more about all those people who are still waiting to receive the gospel

I've put together a variety resources to help you learn more about the many unreached people groups around the world.

faroffsaints.com/so-many

ACTION STEP:

Identify one person God has placed in your circle of influence that you could start praying for or courageously begin a relationship with? Ask God to help you take a first step toward them.

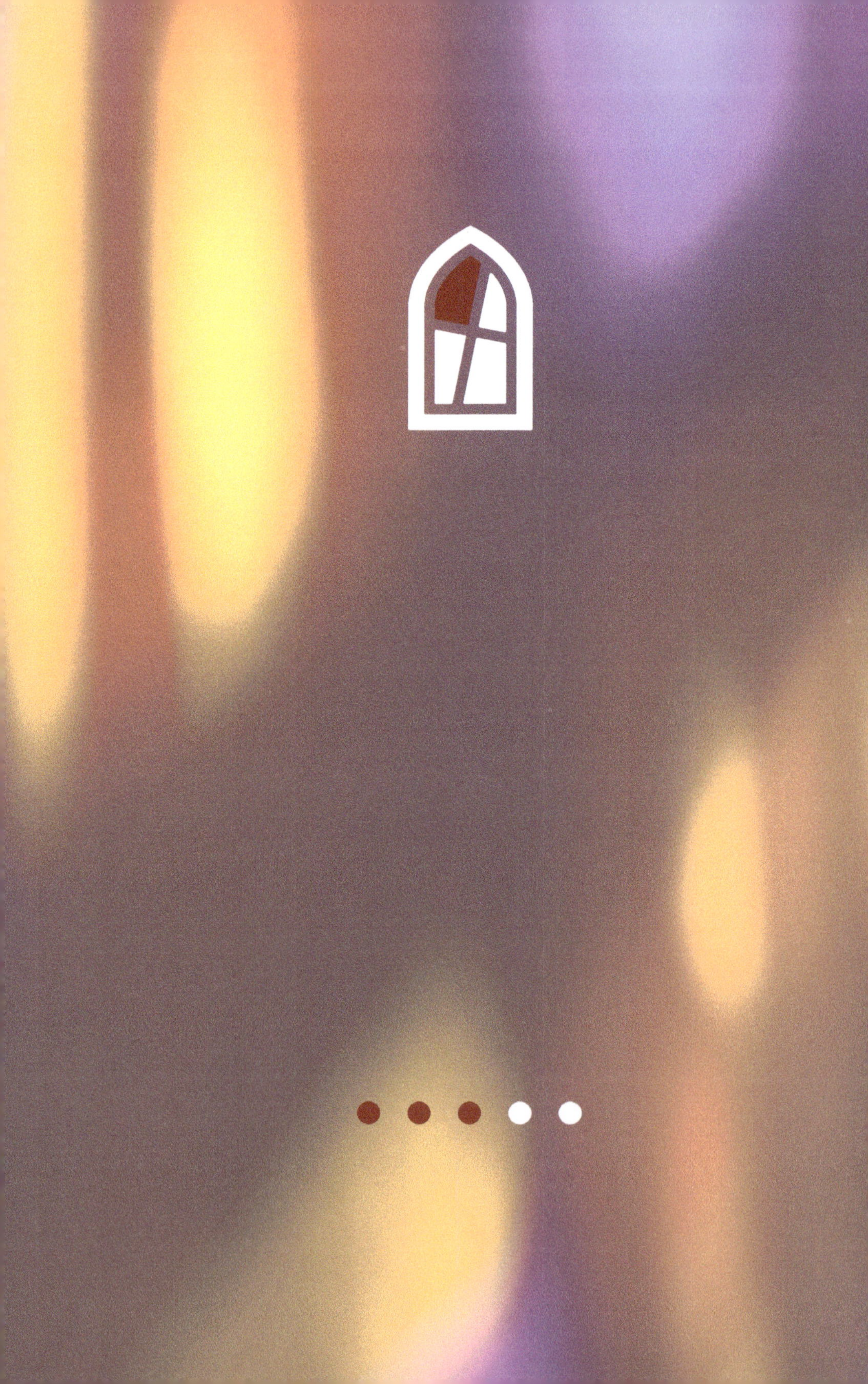

New Things Among Far Off Saints

The wind blows where it wishes, and you hear its sound, but you do not know where it comes from or where it goes. So it is with everyone who is born of the Spirit. John 3:8

So much of what God does is mysterious. His thoughts are above our thoughts and his ways above our ways. Who can know the mind of God? We do see his handiwork at times, however. We catch glimpses of what he is up to as he unfolds his ultimate plan in our time. As we pause to look, we'll find He is hard at work accomplishing his mission.

Following are a few snapshots of God at work through the four M's: Movements, miracles, Muslims and martyrs.

MOVEMENTS

Gospel movements are biblical and required for God's will to be done on earth. Addition is a necessary beginning to reach lost people groups, but only true multiplication will reach the rapidly growing population on our planet. A close reading of Acts 19 reveals five common characteristics of a gospel movement:

1 The gospel spreads spontaneously.

2 Lives are radically transformed.

3 Culture is impacted.

4 Churches are planted.

5 Persecution increases.

Jesus started the first great movement. Though he looked like a failure at the time of his death, he had planted the seeds of a gospel movement in the lives of his followers. As a result, Christianity became the greatest movement in all of human history. We now need ongoing regional movements to consistently take place for the desire of God to be accomplished. Besides those characteristics listed above, there are a few other important facts about movements that are informative:

» Movements almost always start slow and in an unimpressive way. Rarely do you see quick results at the beginning of a true movement.

» It takes a lot of faith and perseverance to see a gospel movement take place. Most of the time, we give up too early.

» Movements must happen among and through the indigenous people in any given location, language or culture.

» Generally, a movement is not a movement until there is consistent reproduction in that people group to the fourth spiritual generation and beyond for both individuals and churches (a convert leads to a new convert, who leads to another convert, who leads to another convert, etc.).

At the turn of the century (year 2000), there was little talk and awareness of gospel movements. Today, many Christian leaders are becoming enlightened that this is a way God may accomplish his big plan. More churches and mission organizations are speaking of and pursuing gospel movements than ever before. In the mission I lead, we are asking God for a gospel movement among every least-reached people group in our generation. When there is an "uncoordinated" awareness that prompts believers and multiple organizations in a unified direction—and if it's biblical—we can surmise that the Holy Spirit is doing a new thing in our day.

MIRACLES

The day of miracles is not past. I'm not talking about the flashy TV healers who gain large followings by their contrived activities, but the quiet, desperate, faith-led miracles that reveal to people who God really is. The Hindu people, who have millions of gods to choose from, are coming to faith in Jesus by the thousands through genuine miracles of God. When this God, by the name of Jesus, can do a miracle that none of their millions of Hindu gods could perform, a powerful message is delivered.

See now that I, I am He, and there is no god besides Me; It is I who put to death and give life. I have wounded and it is I who heals, and there is no one who can deliver from My hand. Deuteronomy 32:39

I have a friend in India named David. He was born Hindu and believed in the Hindu gods. But when his young wife became sick with a brain tumor, no doctor nor Hindu god could heal her. All hope was lost. In desperation, David wept and called out to any god that might hear and any god who might have power to heal this woman he loved. In a matter of hours, there was an unexpected knock on the door. Upon answering the door, David met someone he had never seen before who simply stated, "I was passing by and wanted to ask if I can pray for you." The man prayed for David's wife and she was healed! That was over 45 years ago. Today, David and his wife have led a movement of seeing thousands of churches planted in India among the Hindu people. Miracles continue to be a primary way that God shows up to lead Hindus (and many others) to faith in Jesus.

MUSLIMS

Twenty-two percent of the worlds' population are Muslim (over 1.5 billion). Some people call this the Great Deception since those in Islam are pursuing a favorable standing with Allah, but are instead enslaved in lies, oppression and ongoing rituals of performance. From the Christian perspective, it is a post-Christian religion that has swept over the earth and cast millions of people into the kingdom of darkness.

New things are happening in the world of Islam, however. There have been more gospel movements among Muslim peoples in the last 100 years than in the former 1,500 years combined. More Muslims are having visions of Jesus, creating in them an unresolved longing for truth until that longing is met in Christ. A new hunger for something life-giving is grabbing hold of many of the Muslim peoples.

Since radical Islam raised its ugly head around the world, with Osama bin Laden's Al Qaeda terrorist exploits to Africa's Boko Haram evils, many followers have been asking the simple question, "Is this what I believe?" Extreme Islamist groups are tilling the soil of Muslim hearts, leading to questions that eventually lead to Jesus. In one Muslim region where Muslim background believers have been planting Christian churches for decades, reports indicate the highest response rate among Muslims that they have ever experienced. In their evangelism efforts, among those presented with the full message of the gospel, 11% are deciding to leave Islam and family to become followers of Jesus. That is a staggering statistic, only made possible by a new work of God in these days.

MARTYRS

Precious in the sight of the LORD is the death of his saints. Psalm 115:16

This is the age of martyrs. Between 2005 and 2015, 900,000 believers were martyred for their faith—an average of 90,000 per year. These are stunning numbers which fail to give us a full understanding of how many more are suffering for their faith. Open Doors has concluded that, just in North Korea, there are 70,000 believers in concentration camps suffering for their allegiance to Christ.

So why are we looking at this uncomfortable fact? Let me give you a couple reasons:

1   It's important for us to know the true condition of our spiritual family. These are our fellow brothers and sisters who are suffering for their faith. By the way, did you know that in the book of Acts, 70% of the recorded offerings received were for fellow believers who were suffering?

2   Persecution always shows us that God's Kingdom is advancing. It simply shows us that persecution and martyrdom happen because people will not relinquish their faith in Jesus. Where we see that kind of faith throughout history, we the Kingdom advance significantly.

Consider the early church in Acts:

Saul was in hearty agreement with putting him to death. And on that day a great persecution began against the church in Jerusalem, and they were all scattered throughout the regions of Judea and Samaria, except the apostles. Some devout men buried Stephen, and made loud lamentation over him. But Saul began ravaging the church, entering house after house, and dragging off men and women, he would put them in prison. Therefore, those who had been scattered went about preaching the word. Acts 8:1-4.

In this biblical record, we witness the growth of the church because of persecution and martyrdom as the believers spread to many places that had not yet heard the message about the resurrected Christ.

Iran currently has one of the fastest growing underground church movements in the world. Believers there face intense persecution, many giving their lives for the sake of their new-found faith.

"The persecution of minorities has been a constant under the current Islamic regime in Iran. The Iranian converts to Christianity have been systematically arrested and persecuted as heretics," Mike Ansari, president of Heart4Iran Ministries has stated. Still, with all this persecution, the estimated number of believers in Iran is 800,000 strong. This is still a small 1% minority in a country of 80 million.

One Iranian believer, after moving to America for six months, asked her husband to move them back to Iran. "Why would you want such a thing?" her husband retorted. "It was so awful in Iran! Why do you want to go back?"

"Because I'm being lulled to sleep here," the wife responded. "I'm living in Satan's lullaby. I feel myself falling into a spiritual slumber here in America."

In speaking to any believers in regions where persecution and martyrdom reign, you quickly realize that Christianity is no game or nice cultural choice to adopt. It's a lifestyle that requires steel in your soul, a commitment that costs you and a passion that fuels you. These are powerful entities in the recipe for church vitality and growth.

Those who are far off are experiencing new things from God in unprecedented ways. This is not the time to sleep, but for the church to awake and engage in a great harvest for the glory of God.

"Who can know the mind of God? We do see his handiwork at times, however. We catch glimpses of what he is up to as he unfolds his ultimate plan in our time. As we pause to look, we'll find He is hard at work accomplishing his mission."

 **My Response**

PERSONAL REFLECTION:

Which of the four "M's" get you the most excited? Which one makes you think the most and why?

Learn more about all those people who are still waiting to receive the gospel

I've put together a variety resources to help you learn more about the many unreached people groups around the world.

faroffsaints.com/new-things

OBSERVATION:

See if you can identify "the wind of the Spirit" blowing in your community right now.

ACTION STEP:

Jot down a simple and honest prayer in light of the reading today.

Far Off Saints at Our Doorstep

"When did we see you a stranger and welcome you, or naked and clothe you?"

And the King will answer them, "Truly, I say to you, as you did it to one of the least of these my brothers, you did it to me." Matthew 25:38, 40

We live in a rare time in world history. Never has there been unlimited information at our disposal globally, when communication has been instant, and when the ease and speed of travel has been so prevalent. We have become a global village. The 2020 Coronavirus pandemic demonstrated how interconnected our world has become. Within weeks, the virus had spread to every country and corner on the planet.

Modern technology, new information around the world, a global economy and ease of transportation has caused people everywhere to travel to new places in the world. I can't help but hear the words of Daniel 12:4 in my mind, "But you, Daniel, shut up the words and seal the book, until the time of the end. Many shall run to and fro, and knowledge shall increase." Approximately seven percent of the world's population now live outside their country of birth. This is called the scattering (diaspora) and is being used by God to bring many into his Kingdom that never had an opportunity before. The world has come to us!

SEEING THE FAR OFF SAINTS AMONG US

Consider the story of the Good Samaritan. Jesus told this story to be sure we understand how the importance of living compassionate God-centered lives must happen in the daily interactions of life. Jesus challenges us to notice people in need, change our agenda to address them and make sacrifices to minister to them. Jesus knew how to get to the crux of an issue quickly, didn't he?

In Acts 1:8, Jesus' statement about being witnesses in our Samaria is relevant at this point. Samaria in that day was—well, literally the city of Samaria. The Samaritan people intermarried with gentiles and were considered traitors to Israel and their religious way of life. They were both despised and overlooked. A Samaritan was someone most Jewish people rarely thought worthy of recognition. Their lives did not intersect.

God is stretching his church these days since he's surrounding us with Samaritans. These are the people who are not like us, whose way of thinking we don't understand, whose culture and traditions seem weird, whose language we don't know and whose religion we may despise. But what does God say? "You are to be my witnesses in Samaria."

ONE CHURCH'S STORY

As a pastor in Minnesota for many years, I led a church in a highly diverse neighborhood. Though we were quite inward focused and program-centered when I arrived, years later God impressed on us that we needed to become a highly valued presence in our community. That meant we needed to be intentionally engaged in our community! We began forming relationships with schools in the area, our city government and engaging in community activities that brought us shoulder to shoulder with people much different than us. We began serving the impoverished, ministering to new immigrants, hosting city events in our facilities, and serving in practical ways in our neighborhoods. We didn't do it all right. We made mistakes and we never did achieve what I would call amazing ministry in our community. But something happened to us. Our religion, so easily sequestered to our devotional moments and weekends, had now become more real, daily, sacrificial, risk-taking and fulfilling. As a congregation, we knew we were following God's heart to minister to the Samaritans around us. And something else happened. We became healthy. We began to see new converts... lots of them! In my last two years at this church, we witnessed over 400 far off saints commit their lives to Christ. Praise be to God!

In every church I've served, I've seen something amazing happen when we take risks and simply do what God tells us to do. God is waiting to pour out his blessing and favor on local churches across our nation who commit to courageously and sacrificially serving their Samarias.

>> Over 200 UUPGs (unengaged unreached people groups) have settled in the United States. Remember, these are people groups that have no known believers, no church and no presence of the gospel among them.

>> Many unreached peoples among us are from places we cannot go. God has brought them here.

>> People outside their country of origin are more open to the gospel. This is often the case because people are away from family members who often hold them back, they are exposed to new ideas and religious beliefs they've never heard before and there is an eagerness to start a new life in a new place.

>> There are almost one million international students in the U.S. each year. 80% of them will never be invited into an American's home. 40% of the world's 220 Heads of State once studied in the US.

SOME APPROACHES TO AVOID WHEN MINISTERING CROSS-CULTURALLY

>> Expecting them to come to your church. Don't even invite them (unless you have an extremely unusual church with an over-the-top cultural IQ).

>> Presenting the Four Spiritual Laws or Steps to Peace with God too hastily. Attempting a quick spiritual conversion will usually destroy your opportunity to develop a meaningful long-term relationship and eventually lead them into becoming a disciple of Jesus.

A RELATIONAL APPROACH FOR INFLUENCE

>> Pray for them daily. Have a heartfelt conversation with God about the new people at your doorstep.

>> Ask questions rather than stating facts. Show that you are interested in them and want to know them, what their life has been like, even what they believe. Be a learner.

>> Invite them to your home, especially for holidays and special events. This will help them understand the new culture they are becoming a part of.

>> Ask them if you can pray for some specific needs in their life.

>> Read about their culture and religion so you are informed and aware.

>> Carefully follow the Holy Spirit's leading on what to do and when.

We live in a world that has greatly changed for many of us. We cannot continue to live like we're still in the era when "In God We Trust" was proudly stamped on our currency or when accepted Biblical values permeated our culture. We live in a world where we are surrounded every day by people whose mindset and belief systems are radically different from ours.

Jesus pictured a future day of reward and judgment. It's certainly appropriate to be reminded of it here, since living as Jesus' disciples requires a new way of thinking and acting every single day.

"When did we see you a stranger and welcome you, or naked and clothe you?"

And the King will answer them, "Truly, I say to you, as you did it to one of the least of these my brothers, you did it to me." Matthew 25:38, 40

My Response

PERSONAL REFLECTION:

Jot down one thing God has spoken to you during today's reading. Be specific.

OBSERVATION:

What new thing did you learn in today's reading?

Learn more about all those people who are still waiting to receive the gospel

I've put together a variety resources to help you learn more about the many unreached people groups around the world.

faroffsaints.com/doorstep

ACTION STEP:

What one thing will you do to respond to the world at your doorstep? Keep it simple and attainable.

Challenges to Reaching Far Off Saints

The world of missions is intensely complex. Each culture presents unique challenges with past mission efforts affecting each region positively or negatively: the language barrier, unknown paradigms of thinking, words meaning different things to different people, the unwieldy weight that Americans carry, and strategies that work in one place but don't even get close in another. That's just naming a few of the challenges. They are almost infinite! It is only by the grace of God that Christ's church is established and expanded through global workers as we engage the world. I've given you a short list just to establish the fact that, even for those who make missions their primary focus of ministry, it is incredibly complicated.

I have become all things to all people that by all means I might win some.
1 Corinthians 9:22b.

One of the greatest missionaries in all history, the Apostle Paul, made the above statement. Allow me to make a few brief observations of this revealing verse:

>> Adaptation is required to bring the gospel to lost people.

>> Every person, people group and culture will require new adjustments.

>> The ultimate goal is that we "might win some."

>> The gospel doesn't change, but our methods of delivery must change.

All missions are not created equal. Here's what I mean—doing something in missions is very different than doing the right things. When we engage in missions as individuals or as a church, it is essential that we do so with our eyes wide open, ready to adjust and adapt for the gospel to take root. We must have clarity about what we're attempting to do, face the facts about our engagement and evaluate our effectiveness accordingly.

One of my colleagues, Dr. John Baxter, has stated, "Mission work is always disruptive. We just need to be sure the damage we bring isn't greater than the benefit we leave behind." There are so many things to consider when we think about "becoming all things to all people that we might by all means win some."

SHORT-TERM TRIPS

A short-term mission trip can be a fabulous cross-cultural experience. It opens our eyes to needs around the world, expands our understanding, deepens our gratitude for what we have in America and enriches our lives for-ever. I would never discourage short-term cross-cultural experiences that are done well.

In doing short-term missions, do them with sober intentionality. One church building in Mexico was painted seven times in one summer! This happened because the Mexican pastor wanted to have relationships with Americans and hopefully get funding from them too. The American teams were oblivious, working hard while there and feeling so good about what they did for others. In Belize, the same fifty children accepted Jesus every week when short-term teams came to conduct Bible Schools. Each of these teams went home feeling so good about what they had accomplished, but it wasn't what they imagined. As you can see, short-term missions are not always what they appear.

When planning for a short-term trip, it is essential that there is a win on both sides of the equation. Don't just go and hope you do something of value. Make sure you are legitimately needed. Ask the right and difficult questions early in the planning process. Especially when working with missionaries on location, don't interrupt their work. Find out how you can add value to their goals and objectives.

PARTNERSHIPS WITH NATIONALS

A church may lean towards only supporting nationals, rather than western missionaries. The idea is to get lots of bang for the buck. Just to note here, return on investment (ROI) is not a biblical value, but an American one. It usually does not work well in the goal of global evangelization. It's true that no-one can minister better in a culture than those already in that culture. But remember that I stated missions is complicated. Here are a few examples of just that:

1   Money messes with things.

Pastors and leaders often become servants of the American church because they are receiving funding to sustain their ministry. They feel driven to report what will keep the funds coming and to do the things expected of them. I recently heard of a man robbed and killed because he went to the bank at the same time each month to pick up funds from their US church partners. The money made him a target for violence--even leading to this man's death.

2   There is often minimal accountability.

One very recognized ministry in Asia has excelled at marketing their organization in the West. From what we read and hear in the United States, it seems like a great ministry. In the country they serve, however, they are known for their deception, grossly immoral financial decisions and the divisions it creates among the churches. In the West, thousands of churches and individuals send their monthly donations producing something opposite of what they intend.

3 Lack of sustainability.

If our foreign money funds ministry long-term, it is usually not a wise investment. The most effective ministries I have seen in other countries take place when creative strategies are developed that enable the local church to be self-sustaining. This provides a climate needed for gospel movements to happen and creates ownership of the ministry by the indigenous church in that location.

4 Church partnerships require humble intentionality.

Church partnerships in other places of the world can be a wonderful way to intersect with the greater Body of Christ. The danger for Westerners is the money, prestige and power the American church brings into a relationship. It's difficult to develop these into true partnerships. Good things can come from these relationships, but there must be deliberate attention to leveling the playing field, relating to the sister church as an equal. They often have more to teach and model for us than we have for them.

SOCIAL JUSTICE VS DISCIPLE-MAKING

The greatest injustice in the world is to be born, live, and die and never hear a credible presentation of the gospel. There are many justice issues to address in the world—human trafficking, hunger, child slavery, abuse and marginalization of women, to name a few. These also grieve the heart of God. I am not diminishing these needs nor the godly organizations that address them. In fact, it should never be an either-or proposition. Let us address the world's injustices, but never relinquish our responsibility to address the greatest injustice of them all. Correcting societal injustices can provide doorways to present the gospel to lost people.

A well-drilling team changed lives in significant ways by the water they provided to remote communities. What a gift this was for these people. Yet, with people dying from bad water, they overlooked a strategy to give them the water of life. They impacted their earthly lives but overlooked eternity.

THE KINGDOM OF GOD IN A DESTITUTE SLUM

Rohtak, India is a city northwest of New Delhi in northern India. It resides in a highly unreached area that is 88% Hindu—the others being Sikh and Muslim. On the edge of the city were the dregs of Rohtak, a small slum for this country, but still holding several thousand squatters living a day-by-day survival. Some Indian pastors and I went to visit a church recently planted there.

Walking with my Indian brothers into one end of the compound, I was assaulted by the smell of sewage, garbage and blowing dust all combined. The landscape consisted of small huts made of stick frames or bamboo with retrieved tarps, plastic bags, cardboard, or anything that could give some overhead protection against the sun and occasional rain. The "high-end" homes had weathered wood pallets creatively integrated into the design. Families and friends were together in various sized groups, chatting, laughing and making the best of the day. I noticed that many, especially the children, had hair caked thick with dust. I was told they had little water--not enough for baths or washing, only for drinking. Though I had been in numerous slums before, the cultural shock hit me again as I intermittently reflected on my beautiful house, quality lifestyle and unlimited resources back home. This experience was twisting my soul again.

The children were precious. I began taking photos of several with my phone. Though I couldn't speak their language, they were ecstatic with the interaction. So was I. It was so good to hear their giggles when they viewed themselves, their excited Hindi chatter and smiles so captivating that I still see them clear in my mind ten years later. The group quickly grew from a handful of children to a crowd, all laughing, jumping, some shouting, all grateful that a person from "the outside" noticed them on this day. They have been imprinted on my heart.

One other thing will never be forgotten amidst the squalor of the slum: the church building. It was constructed to be a visible presence, helping people seek God through their intense suffering of poverty. Like the homes, the little worship center was made of crooked branches, though sturdy and well-constructed. Sun-bleached tarps covered the flat roof and sides of this simple structure. One needed to step down a couple steps into a lower hard dirt floor of the 10 by 15 foot gathering room. That's all it was. Nothing else, except a mahogany brown wood pulpit at the far end. It caught my eye because there was something painted on it in English. I'm still perplexed that my language was in their church when no-one could speak it. But there it was! — The Kingdom of God.

A powerful biblical truth hit me in that moment: when the Kingdom of God comes, everything changes even when nothing changes. These Rohtak slum-dwellers still lived in the putrid squalor of their marginalized society, desperately in need of basic life necessities like food, water, clothing and shelter. But they now had hope. Jesus was here! The Kingdom of God had come.

When we think of missions, the church must always be doing what only the church can do. No other organization, institution or entity in the entire world can bring the presence of Jesus. The church can do many good things, but it must always be sure to bring what only the church can provide. All who are far off need exactly that.

"It is only by the grace of God that Christ's church is established and expanded through global workers as we engage the world."

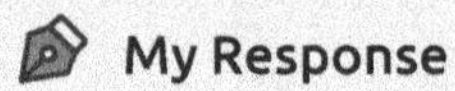 My Response

PERSONAL REFLECTION:

After reading today's section, describe your feelings (i.e. angry, guilty, reflective, defensive, convicted...). And why do you feel this way?

OBSERVATION:

What stands out to you most about the issues addressed today—and why?

Learn more about all those people who are still waiting to receive the gospel

I've put together a variety resources to help you learn more about the many unreached people groups around the world.

faroffsaints.com/challenges

ACTION STEP:

How will you prepare to do the right thing in the right way to help reach those far off?

WEEK ONE TAKE AWAY:

Of all you read and experienced in Far Off Saints this week, what one truth will you embrace or action will you take?

SMALL GROUP MATERIALS

Who Are the Far Off Saints?

GETTING STARTED: (10 MINUTES)

Spend a little time mingling and getting to know your Far Off Saints group members.

Begin with prayer, dedicating these four weeks of the Far Off Saints experience to the Lord. Ask him to do something new in each of your lives these days.

BREAKING THE ICE: (10 MINUTES)

From our Far Off Saints readings so far in week one, what has captured your attention or challenged you significantly? Explain if possible.

VIDEO TEACHING: (30 MINUTES)

» Watch Video #1, <u>Beautiful Feet</u>

» What spoke to you the most in today's teaching?

» Follow up Question: How do you feel about having beautiful feet? (That is, helping to bring the gospel to those who still haven't heard.) For example, do you feel challenged, uncertain, afraid, humbled, etc.?

SCRIPTURE STUDY (30 MINUTES):

Romans 15:8-13; 18-21:

1 Read verses 8-9a: What does this tell you about God? His plan for the world?

2 Read verses 9-13, remembering this was written to Roman Gentiles. How do you think the Romans felt when they read or heard this?

3 Read verses 18-19: Note that Paul's objective was "to bring the Gentiles to obedience." Talk about each of the three ways he pursued this goal and what these really were.

 » By word and deed

 » By the power of signs and wonders

 » By the power of the Spirit of God

Looking at the last part of verse 19, how effective were these three means of the gospel for Paul? Could it be that effective for us? Why or why not?

4 Read verses 20-21: What does it take to make something your ambition? Be as specific as possible.

5 Since Paul made the unreached (those who have never heard the name of Jesus) his ambition, how does this challenge you or frustrate you— or something else?

CONCLUSION: (10 MINUTES)

> » What is your take-away from this evening? (That is, what is your next step with what you've heard and experienced?)

> » Close in prayer, asking God to continue to open your minds and hearts for what he has for each member of the group.

The Revelation Promise

And the gospel must first be proclaimed to all nations. Mark 13:10

Baptists don't generally dance. They did on this night.

A few of us were in a remote region of Asia. We heard of a new church planted a six-hour walk away where there had never been a church before. We didn't know their language, cultural customs, depth of spirituality or style of worship. We only knew that there was a new church planted out there somewhere through the rugged mountains. They were making the six-hour walk to meet us and tell their story. When they arrived, there was much excitement. Some were old, more were young, men, women, boys and girls. About 25 had made the trek. Donning cultural apparel unique to their tribe, they beamed with smiles on their faces, energized that they could meet believers from far away. They didn't have many of these opportunities.

The interpreter relayed their story of hearing about Jesus. The Holy Spirit had opened their minds and hearts to embrace him completely. One by one, their tribe and families were being transformed by the living Christ. With such gratitude for God's grace upon them, dancing became a major way they expressed worship to God. Of course, that's biblical—"Let them praise his name with dancing!" Psalm 149:3 declares. Having brought along some musical instruments that none of us were familiar with, they began playing and dancing. With enthusiasm! And then they started approaching us stoic evangelicals from America to get off the floor and join them! It was hilarious—and beautiful. At one moment, I paused to take it all in. There, in this remote region of Asia, non-dancers were dancing with people that appeared to be out of National Geographic, praising God and celebrating the oneness in Christ we have together. Far off saints brought near by the blood of Christ, worshiping God without inhibition because of the inheritance we have as one.

Worship may seem impractical to us. Most of us immediately have a picture in our mind or a feeling in our heart when we hear the word "worship". It's not always accurate to the biblical definition. One thing we can be sure about worship is that it is central to God's plan for mankind.

> » "...the Father is seeking such people to worship him," John 4:23b.

> » "Oh come, let us worship and bow down; let us kneel before the Lord, our Maker!" Psalm 95:6.

> » "All the nations you have made shall come and worship before you, O Lord, and shall glorify your name," Psalm 86:9

Worship is not about God needing us. It's about us needing God. We were created for an intimate relationship with God, one in which we understand the immense nature and beauty of our Creator and respond appropriately. Our humanness will never be whole until the hole in our heart is filled with an authentic and deep connection with God. We all need to become true worshippers who worship in Spirit and truth to be whole, fulfilled, and at peace. God designed that in us. We were created for this!

That's why Jesus said, the gospel must first be preached to all nations. Everyone needs the opportunity to be whole by being in an intimate relationship with their Creator.

Still, so many around the world—many right around us—have never heard a simple presentation of God and his expressed love for them.

That's what the Revelation Promise is all about. God has determined that this good news will reach every corner of his creation and every segment of humanity will worship him here, near and far off.

The Revelation Promise Includes Everybody

"Susan, you need to come and see this! Quickly!" I shouted to my wife in hushed tones. "You need to see what these children are doing!"

We were on the outskirts of a city in Japan staying in a country home along a small road. As morning arrived, so did the children as they made their way to school. They must have been between the ages of seven and ten. They came in trickles, sometimes one or two at a time—on occasion more, all of them very cutely adorned in Japanese-style garb. But every child did the same thing as they came to our corner. They turned and bowed in reverence to something at the edge of the field across the road, swung forward again to continue their trek to school.

After the children had passed, I walked out to see what it was they were worshiping. I was stunned to see a little family of common clay trolls painted in subdued colors sitting on the ground facing the road. In the past, I had chuckled at these types of humorous figurines, thinking they're a little silly and slightly homely. But these children bowed in respect to these man-made ornaments.

We are wired to worship. We worship things, man-made objects, people, self-designed religions and false gods, and sometimes we worship ourselves. We will worship something because we are wired to worship. We see this throughout Scripture, too. Of course, we are designed to worship God, but our sinful nature leads us in all sorts of desperate directions.

The Revelation Promise is all about an ultimate future worship experience with a massive mosaic of unique people physically before the throne of God and the Lamb.

"Worthy are you to take the scroll and to open its seals, for you were slain, and by your blood you ransomed people for God from every tribe and language and people and nation, 10 and you have made them a kingdom and priests to our God, and they shall reign on the earth." Revelation 5:9-10

"After this I looked, and behold, a great multitude that no one could number, from every nation, from all tribes and peoples and languages, standing before the throne and before the Lamb, clothed in white robes, with palm branches in their hands, and crying out with a loud voice, 'Salvation belongs to our God who sits on the throne, and to the Lamb!'" Revelation 7: 9-10

John, the human author of Revelation, was given a divine glimpse into the future. He is relaying a snapshot of what he saw and describes in some detail this ah-hah moment and the specifics that we need to know. This is not a wish, but an actual picture of a future event in time that will take place.

Did you notice the four words describing the crowd of worshippers? The four descriptors are also in Revelation 5:9-10. These must be significant to what John saw. Though arranged in differing order, God shows us that these people will be from every nation, tribe, people, and language.

Let's investigate these descriptors a bit:

>> **Nation** – from the Greek word "ethnos," meaning a multitude or group residing together with commonalities. It is most often used for Gentiles (non-Jewish peoples) and refers to a race or people cluster of

similar origin. This is not referring to our modern geo-political nations with borders, but people who have common heritage and genealogies that most often group together into identifiable segments of society.

» **Tribe** – from the Greek word "fula," meaning the descendants of a family group. With a tribe, there is an identifiable head, as in the 12 tribes of Israel, and often have unique family characteristics or cultural distinctives. With this word, God actually breaks down the more general reference of "nation" into smaller groups that God clearly recognizes as valuable. The two smallest indigenous tribes in the world are in the Brazilian Amazon Basin--the Kanoê (five people) and the Akuntsu (four people). Tribes can be very small, but God notices every single one.

» **Peoples** – from the Greek word "laos," meaning a group of people residing together in similar localities and conditions. "Laos" is people together that could be from various nations or tribes residing in the same place and conditions, most often seen today in cities where people from many backgrounds cluster together and learn to live together. Wherever they may be living together, God notices them and longs for their salvation as a group of people. This would encourage the Church to pursue global urban ministries, for instance

» **Language** – from the Greek word "glossa" which literally means tongue. It is often understood to mean the language most naturally spoken by someone. People groups and cultures most often form around the language spoken since communication is the most basic entity of forming a common society together. This would reference the fact that every people group and the cultures they represent matter deeply to God.

God's missional fulfillment will not be complete until every grouping of people in the world hears and responds to the gospel of Jesus Christ. As

Habakkuk 2:14 states, "For the earth will be filled with the knowledge of the glory of the LORD as the waters cover the sea."

Jesus also addressed this promise when his disciples asked him, "What will be the sign of your coming and of the end of the age?" Matthew 24:3b. Jesus responded by telling them to watch for wars and rumors of wars, famines and earthquakes. But, Jesus clarified, "that is not the end." He went on to describe how they would be persecuted, suffer terribly, and some would die. Grasp this now: Jesus was telling them that there would be times ahead when it would feel like the end, but it would not be the end. There would be times when they would wish it were the end, but it would not be the end. Jesus then made the clearest statement in all of Scripture about the trigger-point of his coming and the end of this age:

> *This gospel of the kingdom shall be preached in the whole world as a testimony to all the nations (ethne') and then the end will come. Matthew 24:14.*

Here's what Jesus is conveying to us: God has a commitment to every people group in the world to such a degree that he is delaying his return until every people group has heard and responded to the gospel of Jesus Christ.

The Revelation Promise is simply this: God has determined that members from every segment of humanity will be transformed by Christ and worship before the throne of God.

This promise catapults the mission of God for all peoples to the pinnacle of God's plan. All our work and witness point to this ultimate objective. This means:

>> If this is important to God, it must be important to us.

>> If God is delaying his return until all hear, we speed his return by finishing the task.

"The Revelation Promise is all about an ultimate future worship experience with a massive mosaic of unique people physically before the throne of God and the Lamb."

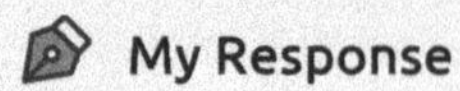 My Response

What most captured your heart today? Why?

What was a new insight for you from the Revelation Promise?

God is gathering saints from every corner of the globe

I've put together a variety resources that I think will be a great encouragement to you. God is at work in the world. Check out these stories!

faroffsaints.com/everybody

ACTION STEP:

Is there anything God is prompting you to do or address right now? Jot that down in the space provided.

The Revelation Promise Reveals a Missionary God

The term "missionary" refers to an individual who responds to God's call on their life to sacrificially bring the gospel to those without it. Missions have changed so much over the years with our speed and ease of travel, instant communication, unlimited online resources, ability to network endlessly and the world's people coming to us like never before. In truth, the traditional model of a missionary, though still needed in many contexts, is not the only way to get missions done today. Innovation is needed and will bear much fruit for the Kingdom.

Still, to see a good, more traditional missionary in action is to witness something of beauty. I'm humbled and inspired by the life and sacrifices of an effective missionary. To reach lost people with the gospel, the global worker steps into another world. They wear their clothes, engage in their culture, speak their language, eat their food, understand their psyche, and sacrifice daily. This is how they express value and love to those they've gone to reach. Stresses of missionary life are extreme and can result in strained marriages, shoestring budgets and culturally unrooted children. If you haven't thanked a missionary lately for their service and sacrifice, today would be a good day. They pay a high price for the call of God in their lives.

Jesus was a missionary in every way. He stepped into our world, spoke our language, ate our food, wore our clothes, understood our psyche, engaged with the culture, and sacrificed daily. In this way, He showed how much He valued and loved us. He took no advantages that as Creator He could have easily arranged. He was born in a barn, a refugee in Egypt, a resident of the pagan city of Nazareth (it was a military town of Rome), of a working class family whose father died at a fairly young age, and had no great physic or impressive looks ("...he had no stately form or majesty that we should look at him, and no beauty that we should desire him," Isaiah 53:2b). Hebrews 4:15 states about Christ, "We do not have a high priest who is unable to sympathize with our weaknesses, but one who in every respect has been tempted as we are, yet without sin." Jesus became one of us to reach us. He was a cross-cultural missionary to the most extreme degree.

Let's consider a few specifics about what "the Word made flesh" did among us as a missionary God:

1   He was relentless about His objective. Jesus was crystal clear about what He came to do. Jesus stated it clearly to His disciples when they were getting a little foggy on their mission, "For even the Son of Man came not to be served but to serve, and to give his life as a ransom for many," Mark 10:45. Nothing distracted Jesus from his mission, not even the well-meaning masses who offered a compelling option that would have avoided the cross. John 6:15 states, "Perceiving then that they were about to come and take him by force to make him king, Jesus withdrew again to the mountain by himself."

2   He implemented a strategic long-term approach. The fact that Jesus had a very limited time to accomplish His work only accentuates the value of Jesus' strategy. Knowing that multiplication always accomplishes more than addition in the long run, Jesus invested

deeply into twelve—and then another 58 (with a total of 70) to a lesser degree. By human standards, Jesus looked like a failure on the day of His death, but the resulting impact of choosing twelve to replicate Himself in them proved to be a world-changing achievement. Jesus knew that to reach the world, multiplication was essential.

3　He showed compassion for the marginalized. Jesus was notorious for being a friend of tax gatherers and sinners. This was a reference to the rare collection of extremely unacceptable friends with whom Jesus spent His time. Among those were the Samaritans (despised by the Jews for being renegade half-breeds), lepers, party-goers, the sick and lame, the demon-possessed, Roman soldiers, and women of bad reputation. Though His primary mission was to call sinners to repentance, Matthew 9:36 records, "When he saw the crowds, he had compassion for them, because they were harassed and helpless, like sheep without a shepherd." Matthew 14:14 tells us, "When he went ashore, he saw a great crowd, and he had compassion on them and healed their sick." God's love oozed out of Him onto the neediest around Him.

4　He broke social mores to embrace foreigners. Those that Jesus embraced were often not of the house of Israel, but seekers from the reprobate nations among them. Consider these as a few samples:

»　A Canaanite woman begged Jesus to heal her demon-possessed daughter. Though the disciples wanted to send her away as a temporary distraction on a busy day, Jesus perceived a seed of faith. Engaging her in conversation about bread and dogs, He rewarded her faith with a miraculous healing as "her daughter was healed from that very hour," Matthew 15:21-28.

»　The first recorded evangelist in Scripture was a Samaritan woman who lived a sinfully loose lifestyle. Because Jesus engaged this outcast in conversation, she came to understand who Jesus was. She gave witness that, "He told me all the things I have done," and led many in the city of Sychar to faith in Christ, John 4:1-42.

» A Roman centurion (soldier of significant rank) pleaded for Jesus to heal his paralyzed servant. With authentic humility, the soldier communicated that he did not deserve for Jesus to "come under my roof", but as one with authority, Jesus would only need to speak the word and the miracle would be accomplished. "I tell you the truth," Jesus exclaimed, "I have not found anyone in Israel with such great faith," Luke 7:1-10. A parallel account records Jesus' statement concerning the Israelite nation and the nations of the world, "I tell you, many will come from east and west and recline at table with Abraham, Isaac, and Jacob in the kingdom of heaven, while the sons of the kingdom will be thrown into the outer darkness. In that place there will be weeping and gnashing of teeth," Matthew 8:11-12. Jesus broke all the norms of that culture and religion to give life to those from other families and nations of the earth. This was revolutionary! It was a shadow of things to come. Jesus was providing an example for His disciples to follow.

5 He designed this kingdom for everyone. After Jesus' death and resurrection, He appeared to two men on the Road to Emmaus. Scripture tells us that their "hearts were burning within them," Luke 24:32, as the mysterious fellow traveler explained the Scriptures concerning the recent events in Jerusalem. When "their eyes were opened" to recognize this stranger to be Jesus, these two ran back to Jerusalem and found the remaining eleven disciples gathered, along with a few others. They needed to know that Jesus was alive! And then Jesus "stood in their midst." He then went on to "open their minds to understand the Scriptures" telling them that "repentance for forgiveness of sins should be proclaimed in His name to all the

nations, beginning from Jerusalem," Luke 24:45-47. Now that His disciples understood the full truth and witnessed the power of the gospel, they recognize that the whole world needs this good news. Of course, Jesus' last words only emphasize the critical nature of this command to all of us left behind as He told us to be His "witnesses in Jerusalem and Judea and Samaria and to the end of the earth," Acts 1:8.

God's actions as a missionary-God accentuate His determination that all the peoples of the world would know, love and follow Jesus. We are here to carry on this critical Kingdom task, "For God did not send his Son into the world to condemn the world, but in order that the world might be saved through Him," John 3:17.

My Response

PERSONAL REFLECTION:

Which of the above characteristics of Jesus do you admire the most and why?

OBSERVATION:

What new or fresh truth about God landed with you today?

God is gathering saints from every corner of the globe

I've put together a variety resources that I think will be a great encouragement to you. God is at work in the world. Check out these stories!

faroffsaints.com/missionary-god

ACTION STEP:

Write a simple prayer in gratitude for God being a Missionary God for you.

The Revelation Promise Aligns Our Heart

For one will scarcely die for a righteous person—though perhaps for a good person one would dare even to die—but God shows his love for us in that while we were still sinners, Christ died for us. Romans 5:7-8

I love worshiping with my son, Shane. He feels things so deeply. Many times, while engaged in singing or prayer, I've seen the involuntary tears of adoration running down his face—and then mine started. Seeing into his heart not only endears me to him, but helps me to see who he really is, inspiring me to enthusiastically worship with him. Something powerful happens when we look into the heart of another.

This is also true of God. If we know His heart, we are drawn to Him in a way that elicits an authentic response of adoration, allegiance, and obedience. We need to move beyond factual and intellectual knowledge of God into an experiential knowledge of Him. Something profound and miraculous happens when we sincerely experience the heart and love of God.

So what is unique about God's heart and his way of loving us?

God's love extends to everybody. Expressing His deepest desires and motivations, these sample texts give us insight into God's heart:

>> 1 Chronicles 16:24, "Declare his glory among the nations, his marvelous works among all the peoples!"

>> Psalm 96:1-3, "Oh sing to the Lord a new song; sing to the Lord, all the earth! Sing to the Lord, bless his name; tell of his salvation from day to day. Declare his glory among the nations, his marvelous works among all the peoples!"

>> Psalm 22:7, "All the ends of the earth shall remember and turn to the Lord, and all the families of the nations shall worship before you."

>> One of my favorite Old Testament scriptures that reveals God's heart is found in Psalm 67, where the chorus states, "Let the peoples praise you, O God, let all the peoples praise you!" That word for "peoples" in the Hebrew most literally means people groups. This is a statement declaring God's love for every people group in the world in an era when most people thought He only loved the nation of Israel. This reveals the heart of God for even the remotest overlooked people group in the world.

Even though the above Scriptures are declarations by various writers, remember that God is the author. Through these writers, He is revealing His desire for all the peoples of the world.

God's love found a way. When God called Abram out among all people on earth, he told him, "In you, all the families of the earth shall be blessed," Genesis 12:3b. This was not some generic blessing the Creator would lay on people, but a calculated strategy so that all the people groups of the world would know, experience, and worship God. There is no greater blessing than this. This promise would come through the life and family of Abraham, which eventually became the nation of Israel. One way that we are impacted by this is that the Scriptures have been written and handed down through the family of Abraham, the Jewish people, profoundly impacting and blessing the whole world.

Twenty-three times in the book of Ezekiel we read the phrase, "Then they will know that I am the Lord." Each time, God is referring to actions He will take to prove to various nations of the world that He is Lord. These tribes and nations would be enlightened to understand that there is no god like Jehovah. God does some fairly radical things to show the world who He is so they have the choice to place their allegiance in Him. These actions are not restricted within the record of Ezekiel, of course. We see God's power demonstrated to Egypt in the plagues and the parting of the Red Sea, through the repentance and subsequent grace of God toward Nineveh, and shepherd David's surprising defeat of Goliath as the overconfident Philistine army looked on in stunned amazement. God was making His name famous in the world so that all the peoples of the earth would wrestle with the reality and greatness of our Creator God.

God's love is profoundly sacrificial. J. Edwin Hartill, my professor of Bible at Northwestern College in St. Paul, Minnesota, often shared his thoughts about Scripture's best-known verse, John 3:16:

God—*the greatest lover,*
So loved—*the greatest degree,*
The world—*the greatest number,*
That He gave—*the greatest act,*
His only Son—*the greatest gift,*
So that everyone—*the greatest invitation,*
Who believes—*the greatest simplicity,*
In Him—*the greatest person,*
Will not perish—*the greatest escape,*
But—*the greatest difference,*
Have—*the greatest certainty,*
Eternal life—*the greatest destiny.*

Remember now, that "one will scarcely die for a righteous person—though perhaps for a good person one would dare even to die—but God shows his love for us in that while we were still sinners, Christ died for us," Romans 5:7-8. God did this for an undeserving world! His love extends to the nations that have rejected him, the peoples that have ignored Him, and the masses that have not heard of Him. God's heart is revealed through His declared Word, strategic actions, and compelling sacrifice for ALL the peoples of the world. God's heart of love extends to them all.

If you really love someone, you love who they love. When our daughter Bethany was a little girl, she once left Teddy at Grandma's house hundreds of miles away. She was terribly distraught. For a moment—and only a moment—I thought about the $10 value of Teddy and how easy it would be to quickly replace him. Thankfully, that thought quickly vanished. A quick call to Grandma and Teddy was soon on his way to our home, gently tucked in a box with a grandma's touch, even with a small blanket and pillow for Teddy's comfort. Without our daughter's love, Teddy was just a stuffed animal that could be easily replaced, but with our daughter's love, he became deeply valued. We needed to treat Teddy like Bethany did. When you love someone, you love who they love. That's how you love that person.

Do you want to really love God? Love who He loves. He's made it very clear who that is. It's an important piece of being in alignment with God and fulfilling our part in the Revelation Promise.

"If we know His heart, we are drawn to Him in a way that elicits an authentic response of adoration, allegiance, and obedience. We need to move beyond factual and intellectual knowledge of God into an experiential knowledge of Him. Something profound and miraculous happens when we sincerely experience the heart and love of God."

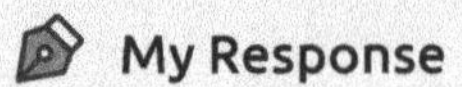 My Response

PERSONAL REFLECTION:

On a scale of 1 to 10, how do you rate your act of loving God by loving who he loves? Why this rating?

OBSERVATION:

Why do you think it's so common to overlook the peoples of the world who God loves?

God is gathering saints from every corner of the globe

I've put together a variety resources that I think will be a great encouragement to you. God is at work in the world. Check out these stories!

faroffsaints.com/heart-surgery

ACTION STEP:

Ask God to bring to mind a person you can love on God's behalf. Now, jot their name down along with a simple first step you can take to do that.

The Revelation Promise Points Us to God's Agenda

My Dad had a tendency to say things over and over, especially when he was concerned we didn't hear it the first time. When we heard a theme repeated until we were sick of it, we took notice. This was something very important to him and he expected us to respond accordingly.

Our Heavenly Father does the same thing for us. When He states something over and over, take note! He's making sure we don't miss an expected responsibility He wants us to take action on.

Many books have been written on this topic, so what I'll share with you here is a Cliff-notes version at best. Let's call it a preface. However, I hope the Scriptures will speak to you in a way that moves you to action—something our Heavenly Father is desperately wanting from all of us.

We may already know about various versions of the Great Commission (Matthew 28:18-19, Mark 16:15-18, Luke 24:45-49, Acts 1:6-8). Understand that these were Jesus' last words before His departure. They hold extra "weight" in our consideration. They all emphasize three critical truths:

1   **God will empower us to do His will.** The Holy Spirit is essential for us to accomplish His mission. We cannot accomplish it through

human effort, ingenuity, or technology. God's mission can only be achieved through Holy Spirit power. And when we are empowered by God, we will be engaged in His global mission. His Spirit moves us into this because this is His burning determination.

2 **We are to be witnesses.** When a witness is in a courtroom, they don't need to be an expert at anything. They only need to tell what they have seen, heard and experienced. Yes—there are expert witnesses, too. They are the doctors, forensic experts, and psychologists that can speak deeply and insightfully into the issues at hand. In the Christian realm, those expert witnesses are those with the gift of evangelism (considered to be about 10% of believers). All of us are to be general witnesses, however. This is basic and essential to what it means to be a Jesus follower.

3 **This good news is to reach every people group in the world.** In recent decades, the church at large has overlooked the central theme of the Great Commission. It calls us not only to make disciples, but specifically that we be determined to disciple every people group in the world (ethne). This global dimension of ministry is not to be an add-on or something we work towards after we get our act together on our home turf. God intends for this activity to be a part of our DNA as disciples of Jesus and central to our function and priorities of His church.

The book of Romans is widely considered as the theology text of the New Testament. It is deep, profound, and compelling. Did you know that Romans has missional bookends? Did you realize that this theological treatise of the New Testament is all about spreading the gospel to every people group in the world? In his brief word of greeting and introduction, the writer of Romans states that the purpose of this letter is to "bring about the obedience of faith for the sake of his name among all the nations," Romans 1:5b. Don't miss the "all the nations" part. This is the very intention of this letter to Rome. Bookend left.

As the writer of Romans is concluding his teaching, he revisits the central purpose of this letter: to be sure this mystery of salvation is "known to all nations, according to the command of the eternal God, to bring about the obedience of faith," Romans 16:26. Yes—Romans was written to be sure that every ethne of the world will know and experience this "obedience of faith" to our Lord and Savior, Jesus Christ. Bookend right.

Allow me to highlight one small section of Romans, chapter 10:11-15:

For the Scripture says, "Everyone who believes in him will not be put to shame." For there is no distinction between Jew and Greek; for the same Lord is Lord of all, bestowing his riches on all who call on him. For "everyone who calls on the name of the Lord will be saved."

How then will they call on him in whom they have not believed? And how are they to believe in him of whom they have never heard? And how are they to hear without someone preaching? And how are they to preach unless they are sent? As it is written, "How beautiful are the feet of those who preach the good news!"

Did you know that best research today reveals that there are still around 7,000 unreached people groups (UPGs) in the world? (from PeopleGroups.org)

An unreached people group is a people group among which there is no indigenous community of believing Christians with adequate numbers and resources to evangelize their own people without outside (cross-cultural) assistance. [Missions and You! Larry W. Caldwell, 2009, p.9)

Did you know that there are still around 3,000 unengaged unreached people groups (UUPGs) in the world? (from PeopleGroups.org) These are people groups with no known believers and no one working among them to establish Christ's church.

Suddenly, the statement from Romans 10 takes on critical importance:

How then will they call on him in whom they have not believed? And how are they to believe in him of whom they have never heard? And how are they to hear without someone preaching? And how are they to preach unless they are sent? As it is written, "How beautiful are the feet of those who preach the good news!"

No one will bring them the gospel except followers of Jesus. Unfortunately, for over 2,000 years we have fallen short in accomplishing this task. We are called by God to either go or send. It is central to God's plan for believers and his agenda for the world.

"When He states something over and over, take note! He's making sure we don't miss an expected responsibility He wants us to take action on."

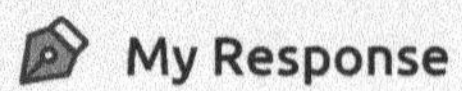 My Response

How well are you tracking with God's agenda right now?

Why do you think there are still so many unengaged and unreached people groups in the world?

God is gathering saints from every corner of the globe

I've put together a variety resources that I think will be a great encouragement to you. God is at work in the world. Check out these stories!

faroffsaints.com/gods-agenda

ACTION STEP:

What action could you take to obediently step into God's agenda? Then, write a brief prayer to God about what you want to do in response to his plan.

The Revelation Promise Clarifies Our Mission

One of my favorite movie series is Mission Impossible. Tom Cruise is invincible as he catapults 30 feet from roof-top to roof-top, remains submerged underwater longer than any normal human could, and triumphantly pulls off the mask to complete his elusive capture and ultimate victory. All of this because he is on a mission—he's pursuing an objective that he and his team will do anything to achieve.

When Jesus left planet Earth, he declared the mission we are to be on:

"Go therefore and make disciples of all nations, baptizing them in the name of the Father and of the Son and of the Holy Spirit," Matthew 28:19.

Most of us are so familiar with this scripture that we don't see what it says any more. So, let's dig a bit.

"Go therefore" is a Greek present active participle which actually means, "As you are going...." Jesus is telling us that this mission is to be an ongoing daily lifestyle we're engaged with in whatever we're doing. We are to be Christian Tom Cruises who will do whatever it takes to achieve the objective.

"Make disciples of all nations" literally means, "Disciple the nations." This is critical for us to grasp. Jesus is not telling us to make disciples generally. He is specifically commanding us to engage in spreading the gospel to all the nations of the world. Of course, making disciples (learners, followers, imitators) right where we are needs to be our daily objective, but the Great Commission is primarily about making sure that every person of the world has the opportunity to follow Jesus.

Let's go a step further. The word for "nations" is the Greek word "ethne" from which we get the word "ethnic." Jesus is not even referring to geo-political nations in this command, but to every ethnic people group in the world.

Capture this now—Jesus' last word to His followers, which is of supreme importance, was that they were to disciple all the people groups of the world as a part of their ongoing lifestyle. This is what it means to be "on mission" with God.

When our children were young, we would regularly take long road trips, usually from Minnesota to Texas where some family members lived. When it comes to travel, I get very focused. I am determined to get there as efficiently as possible. As a result, our family adopted a road-trip motto: "drink little, be happy." That's because there would be no extra stops along the way. When we filled up with gas, then and only then were they to take care of their personal business. We were on mission. We had an objective and nothing would distract us from getting that done. Reflecting back now, I recognize it was maybe a little extreme for a road trip. Yikes!

God intends His church and every believer to be on mission. Nothing should distract us from achieving exactly what God has told us to do. However, I'm concerned that many Jesus-followers are a little foggy about what He told us to do. And because we're unsure of our mission, it has remained undone. In fact, God's mission will never get done until we clearly understand what that is, what it takes to get it done, and what our part is in pushing it forward.

One of our sons was a master at joyful disobedience. When Susan and I would leave for a few hours, we would clearly delineate what we expected to happen while we were gone. A simple directive would be something like, "Have your room picked up and dust the living room furniture by the time we come home." Simple enough! Upon our return, our child would joyfully welcome us at the door with a beautiful bouquet of wildflowers for his mother and a warm note of appreciation for His father, but the chores were left unfinished. By the way, this does create a puzzling disciplinary situation.

I'm convinced that we believers often practice joyful disobedience. We do good things, but not the right things. We may feel so smug about the good we've done while overlooking the critical things we've left undone. We are active and wanting to please, but are determined to do it on our terms and in our self-designed way while missing out on the mission of God.

> *After this I looked, and behold, a great multitude that no one could number, from every nation, from all tribes and peoples and languages, standing before the throne and before the Lamb, clothed in white robes, with palm branches in their hands, and crying out with a loud voice, "Salvation belongs to our God who sits on the throne, and to the Lamb!"*
> *Revelation 7:9-10*

This will be the greatest worship service in the history of all creation! People from every division and segment of the human race will be represented as children of God. The final culmination of God's desire and plan will come to fruition. People from every people group, tribe, language, culture and family line—great and small, rich and poor, educated or not, sophisticated and simple, highly literate and completely oral, well-dressed and scarcely dressed—will stand in the presence of God having been redeemed by the blood of the Lamb!

We get to be a part of seeing the Revelation Promise become reality! We are expected to participate in this as disciples of Jesus.

 My Response

PERSONAL REFLECTION:

On a scale of 1 being "not at all" and 10 being "I'm totally focused and engaged", how on mission are you? Why are you at this rating?

OBSERVATION:

Jot down two things a Tom Cruise-type Christian would act like when being on mission.

1

2

God is gathering saints from every corner of the globe

I've put together a variety resources that I think will be a great encouragement to you. God is at work in the world. Check out these stories!

faroffsaints.com/clarity

ACTION STEP:

Identify a way you may be practicing joyful disobedience. Write a brief prayer to God about this.

WEEK TWO TAKE AWAY:

Of all you read and experienced in Far Off Saints this week, what one truth will you embrace or action you will take?

SMALL GROUP MATERIALS

The Revelation Promise

GETTING STARTED: (10 MINUTES)

Spend a little time mingling and catching up with your Far Off Saints group members.

Begin with Prayer, dedicating these remaining three weeks of Far Off Saints to the Lord. Ask him to meet you powerfully as you engage in his Word and with one another today.

BREAKING THE ICE: (10 MINUTES)

From our Far Off Saints readings so far in week two, what has captured your attention or challenged you significantly? Explain if possible.

VIDEO TEACHING: (30 MINUTES)

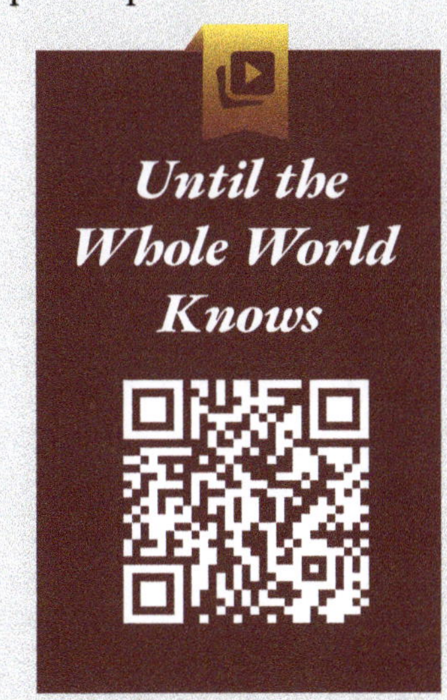

» Watch #2 – <u>Until the Whole World Knows</u>

» What spoke to you most from today's teaching?

» Follow up Question: How do you feel about the ultimate completion of God's plan for all people and your part in it? Be honest about what's stirring in you.

Psalm 67. Read the entire Psalm.

In verse 1, David the Psalmist hopes for God to "be gracious to us and bless us."

- » Why is it okay to want God's grace and blessings?

- » What did this possibly look like in David's time?

- » How might this look in our day?

- » What do you think happens when God's face shines on us?

- » Do you happen to know anyone who obviously has God's grace, blessing, and face shining on them? Explain.

Read verse 2:

- » Why does God bless people? (Along with your answers, notice the "that" at the beginning of this verse.)

- » What do you think is the "your way" that is to be known on earth? And why is this important?

- » How was God's "saving power" demonstrated among all the nations in David's time and now also today?

Read verses 3 and 5: The Psalmist, the man after God's own heart, exuberantly declares his heart-desire.

- » What does this tell you about God?

- » What does this reveal to you about the place of praise and worship in us?

- » How do verses 4 and 6 fit into the theme and flow of this Psalm?

- » How do you see this Psalm relating to the Revelation Promise in Revelation 7:9-10?

- » In what ways do these Scripture passages influence your understanding of God or his redemptive plan for mankind? Explain.

CONCLUSION: (10 MINUTES)

What is your take-away from this evening? (That is, what is your next step with what you've heard and experienced?)

Close in prayer, asking God to continue to open your minds and hearts for what he has for each member of the group.

Could the Church Be Far Off?

On a dangerous seacoast where shipwrecks often occur there was once a crude little life-saving station. It was just a hut, and there was only one boat, but the few devoted members kept a constant watch over the sea; with no thought for themselves, they went out day or night tirelessly searching for the lost.

So many lives were saved by this little station that it became famous. Some of those who were saved, and others, wanted to be associated with the station and give of their time and money to support its work.

New boats were bought, and new crews were trained. The little station grew.

Some of the new members were unhappy with the crude building. They felt the rescued needed a more comfortable place as their first refuge.

The building was enlarged, with nicer furniture. Now the life-saving station became a popular gathering place and was re-decorated beautifully and furnished as a sort of club.

Less of the members were now interested in going to sea on life-saving missions, so they hired lifeboat crews to do this work.

About this time a large ship was wrecked off the coast, and the hired crews brought in boatloads of cold, wet and half-drowned people.

They were dirty and sick, and some of them had black skin, and some spoke a strange language, and the beautiful new club was considerably messed up.

At the next meeting, there was a split in the club membership. Most of the members wanted to stop the club's life-saving activities as being unpleasant and a hindrance to the normal life pattern of the club.

But some members insisted that life-saving was their primary purpose and pointed out that they were still called a life-saving station. But they were finally voted down and told that if they wanted to save the lives of all the various kinds of people who were shipwrecked in those waters, they could begin their own life-saving station down the coast. They did. And the same thing happened to them.

If you visit the seacoast today you will find a number of exclusive clubs along that shore. Shipwrecks are still frequent in those waters, only now most of the people drown.

Written in 1953 by Rev. Dr. Theodore O. Wedel

~

Every church in history has needed to courageously assess and realign itself with God's original plan again and again during its lifespan. That's part of being Christ's church. Could your church be far off? Of course! Or maybe just a little.

In the week ahead, I urge you to open your mind and heart. I encourage you to pray sincerely for God to speak and for you to hear. I challenge you to be bold and courageous as you consider what God has for you and your church. Most of all, pray that God will do what he wants in you so all the world here, near and far off will know that Jesus Christ is Lord.

"Now the life-saving station became a popular gathering place and was re-decorated beautifully and furnished as a sort of club."

What Our Church Ancestry Reveals

But you are a chosen race, a royal priesthood, a holy nation, a people for his own possession, that you may proclaim the excellencies of him who called you out of darkness into his marvelous light. 1 Peter 2:9

CRAZY BIG THINGS IN A SIMPLE LITTLE CHURCH

This was the first church where I was the lead pastor. I was excited about seeing what God would do. After being there only a short time, I learned that there had not been a salvation in that church for 40 years, except for church children who prayed to receive Christ. It was a very happy, small, inward-grown community of believers with little impact on the community in which they resided. This bothered me. A lot.

After a season of seeking the Lord and trying various things—like starting a Saturday evening outreach service—I felt like God wanted us to take a radical step. It was agreed that we would shut down Sunday morning Sunday School and begin prayer groups for lost people. Ending Sunday school was a bit traumatic for many since this is what they had always done. I was convinced, however, that the last thing these people needed was to learn more. They needed to start practicing what they already knew. So, we prayed. The groups prayed together for people by name. Every member of each group wrote down the names of at least five people that needed to know Jesus. Their commitment was to pray for each person by name during the week between their group gatherings.

Our church prayed for nine months. We began to wonder if this was the right thing to do. People asked me, "How long are we going to do this?!" But we kept at it. We just prayed for people by name.

At the nine-month mark, things began to happen. People began to come to faith in crazy ways, some through the people who had been praying for them, others in ways only God could arrange. Every new birth was of people on someone's prayer list. One person who managed a liquor store suddenly had an urge to read the Bible while he was at work. The prompting was so strong, he left work to go home. He found a Bible and began reading. For the next week he called in sick every day and stayed home to read the Bible. He would put it down at times, but only for 15 minutes or so. He couldn't keep his hands off the Word, would pick it up and continue reading. In a week, he read the entire Bible from front to back. When he finished, he fell on his face and asked Jesus to be his Lord and Savior!

In the following six months, that small church of 120 people witnessed 59 first-time decisions for Christ simply because people prayed without ceasing. The church came alive! It was back on mission with God's agenda.

A BIG PLAN WITH A SMALL BEGINNING

Jesus came from Heaven to earth to catalyze God's plan of salvation for all of mankind. Specifically, He came to redeem for Himself a people to carry out his redemptive purposes.

1 Peter 2:9 reveals that God established a new race, priesthood and nation to help the world see who God really is—how outstanding he is above all other gods. This new race and priesthood is called "the Church"—the called out ones.

The beginnings of the Church were initiated with the coming of Jesus when he arrived at the manger in Bethlehem. After all, he is "the head" of the body, the Church. This was the very beginning of the actual establishment of this new people set apart for God.

On the night Jesus was born, the angel made a proclamation to the shepherds on the Bethlehem hillside:

And the angel said to them, "Fear not, for behold, I bring you good news of great joy that will be for all the people. For unto you is born this day in the city of David a Savior, who is Christ the Lord," Luke 2:10-11

Please notice that from the first word of Jesus' arrival there is the clarification that this is for "all the people." Jesus' coming and the establishment of this new nation was intended to be comprehensive—to bring "good news of great joy" to all the peoples of the earth. This reveals to us that God's plan to reach "all the ethne" is not an insignificant segment of God's overall plan. It *is* God's overall plan. Because God was purposeful in stating this from the very first proclamation of Christ's coming, we must grasp its importance.

The birth of the Church is recorded in Acts 2. Among many other things, God is always strategic. He certainly was on Pentecost. We read that "there were dwelling in Jerusalem Jews, devout men from every nation under heaven," Acts 2:5. Along with that, as the Church is being birthed, the Holy Spirit is unleashed among them enabling the disciples to speak in languages they had not learned but were needed for those present to clearly hear and understand this "good news of great joy." I find it fascinating that, on the day the Church is birthed, the main emphasis was not on edifying those who already knew the gospel, not on community life, and not on programs or assuaging preferences or a building or a worship band. It was on proclaiming the gospel to people from every nation under heaven. Take note: this is not accidental. This was God being very strategic. In this activity, God is again helping us to understand the critical function and purpose of the church.

Consider Pentecost, meaning "fiftieth" since it's the 50th day after the Passover when this event occurred. At that time, however, it was still known by the Old Testament name, The Feast of Weeks. This was a special holiday established for Israel by God (Exodus 34:22) to celebrate the first portion of the harvest of wheat "and the feast of ingathering at the year's end." Few Israelites had any understanding that this feast, celebrated for generations, was a picture foretelling the first harvest of the Messiah's Church which would be coming in the future. Again, take note: this was the beginning of the harvest for the Church. And this harvest could only be brought in by the presence and power of the Holy Spirit. This harvest is so significant, the task so big, the complexities so stunning and the urgency so great that we should never attempt this by human effort alone. This harvest activity must be a Holy Spirit led and empowered endeavor every time we engage.

NO PLAN "B"

I love Christ's Church. Having been a pastor for 28 years, I saw the good, the bad and the ugly. I am still amazed that God continues to use his Church as the primary means to accomplish his redemptive plan for the world. I say this, not to mock the Church, but to highlight God's grace toward the Church. We are redeemed people, but we are also broken people. We struggle with sin, not only as individuals, but as local churches too. We easily get caught up in our petty agendas, self-serving activities, ego-feeding endeavors, "righteous" preferences that have nothing to do with holiness, priorities that adhere to culture more than Christ and often measure our successes by the wrong measuring stick. That Christ would not give up on us is a testament to his amazing grace.

This amazing grace is also what makes the Church thrive in all the right ways—by setting captives free, seeing lives radically transformed, neighborhoods influenced, people groups reached, cultures impacted, churches planted and God glorified through the beauty of her obedience. God continues to pour out His grace and power on his redeemed people to see His purposes completed. The Church is God's plan to reach the world with the good news of Jesus. There is no plan "B".

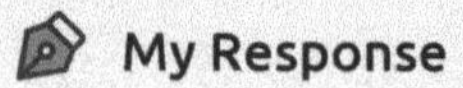 My Response

PERSONAL REFLECTION:

What captured your imagination in the story of the small church having a big impact?

OBSERVATION:

Was there a new insight for you from the announcement of Jesus' birth at Bethlehem?

Every church has room to grow into God's heart for the world

I've put together a handful of resources that I think will challenge you and your church. God has a big vision for the world; we need a big vision too.

faroffsaints.com/ancestry

ACTION STEP:

Jot down the names of five people you can start praying for who need to know Jesus. (I challenge you to share those names with your small group this week.)

1

2

3

4

5

A Model to Follow (Part One)

We can learn so much about the Church from its beginnings. By looking at the very beginning of something, we learn about its intended purpose, plans and objectives. God initiated and shaped the Church early on to accomplish His purposes and be as effective as possible in doing that. We have much to learn by going back to our roots.

Our current day American church looks very different from the early church in the book of Acts. That's not necessarily bad so long as our cultural adaptation has not superseded our biblical alignment. I do wonder, however, what Jesus would say to our churches today if he were to drop in. How penetrating would his analysis be? How far off have we drifted from what really matters to him?

In the name of cultural relevance, we have often elevated a production over Holy Spirit power, marketing over personal evangelism, programs over disciple-making, buildings and equipment over investment in people, and planning over God's leading in the moment. Each of these contrasts are not mutually exclusive. We can have both. I'm just not confident we usually do. The challenge for us immersed in the American church is to realize we, as in every other culture, have manufactured our version of church. It might not be as biblical as we would like to assume.

A quick read of early biblical church history reveals a few outstanding characteristics of the church which will be helpful to acknowledge and wrestle with a bit. I want to highlight three primary observations from the book of Acts:

1   Selfless generosity was a significant factor in how influential the church became.

2   Suffering, signs and wonders were the means of making inroads to unreached people and regions.

3   Strategies of true multiplication enabled the church to see crucial movements take place.

SELFLESS GENEROSITY

The early church was characterized by uncommon sacrificial generosity. Consider Acts 4:32-37:

"³² Now the full number of those who believed were of one heart and soul, and no one said that any of the things that belonged to him was his own, but they had everything in common. ³³ And with great power the apostles were giving their testimony to the resurrection of the Lord Jesus, and great grace was upon them all. ³⁴ There was not a needy person among them, for as many as were owners of lands or houses sold them and brought the proceeds of what was sold ³⁵ and laid it at the apostles' feet, and it was distributed to each as any had need. ³⁶ Thus Joseph, who was also called by the apostles Barnabas (which means son of encouragement), a Levite, a native of Cyprus, ³⁷ sold a field that belonged to him and brought the money and laid it at the apostles' feet."

The first believers in Jerusalem were selfless with everything they could call their own. They were generous with what they owned, their money and their net worth. Many intentionally became less wealthy so those struggling would have their needs met. They were even generous in their testimony of Jesus Christ. We can minimize the significance of this by emphasizing that this was a unique time in history (which it was) or that the climate for new believers thrust them into immediate hardship (which it did). But let's also recognize that they were driven to submit everything they were and all they had to be sure the cause of Christ succeeded. They did this to such a degree that the early believers were characterized by their selfless generosity.

As I understand this, two factors compelled them to be generous:

1   They chose to love one another. They heeded Jesus' words to love their neighbor in ways similar to that of the Good Samaritan.

2   They were committed to the command of Jesus to disciple the nations. The first believers were driven to finish this task. Their own time and possessions were resources for Christ's use.

You may be feeling what I'm feeling—I'm starting to feel a little guilty for what I have and for not wanting to give it all away. It's okay. Our tendency to overvalue temporal things needs to be pressed by God's agenda. Go ahead and wrestle with the tension. Ask God what this may mean for you.

The early church was not only generous with their personal wealth and ownership, they were generous with their people. Consider the thriving church at Antioch in Acts 13:1-3:

Now there were in the church at Antioch prophets and teachers, Barnabas, Simeon who was called Niger, Lucius of Cyrene, Manaen, a lifelong friend of Herod the tetrarch, and Saul. [2] While they were worshiping the Lord and fasting, the Holy Spirit said, "Set apart for me Barnabas and Saul for the work to which I have called them." [3] Then after fasting and praying they laid their hands on them and sent them off.

Did you see it? The Antioch church sent off their very best in response to God's leading. Their very best, by the way, were Saul (soon to be known as Paul, the man who wrote nearly half the New Testament Scriptures) and Barnabas (a courageous and encouraging leader-teacher). These two became the dynamic duo, some of the most effective missionaries ever sent out into the world. The church didn't send out those they wouldn't miss, but the best of the best. The church was ready to sacrifice its own megastars and the seeming potential for impact in their locality. Antioch was not reached yet, either. Still, they made sure ministry was not contained within their local church. This is generosity! It made all the difference in the history of the church and profoundly increased the degree of influence this young church had in the world. Selfless generosity was a significant factor in how influential the church became.

We will continue our investigation of early church characteristics tomorrow.

"I do wonder, however, what Jesus would say to our churches today if he were to drop in. How penetrating would his analysis be? How far off have we drifted from what really matters to him?"

 **My Response**

What do you see in the early church that is attractive to you? Why is this attractive to you?

What impresses you the most about the early church's generosity?

Every church has room to grow into God's heart for the world

I've put together a handful of resources that I think will challenge you and your church. God has a big vision for the world; we need a big vision too.

faroffsaints.com/model-church

ACTION STEP:

How could you obediently respond to the early church's modeling of generosity? (Keep it simple, attainable and sustainable.)

A Model to Follow
(Part Two)

The early believers were amazing people who developed an obedient sacrificial church on mission for Jesus. You can feel it as you read the biblical records. They were God-dependent, captured by a vision and compelled by their love of Jesus. It inspires me every time I read about them.

Today, we will look at two more of the outstanding characteristics of the early church (in addition to yesterday's selfless generosity).

SUFFERING, SIGNS AND WONDERS

Who likes to suffer? And miracles--they are nice in theory, but we certainly don't see them very often these days. So what do these facts mean for us today? Let's investigate a few passages of Scripture related to the early church:

And there arose on that day a great persecution against the church in Jerusalem, and they were all scattered throughout the regions of Judea and Samaria, except the apostles. Now those who were scattered went about preaching the word. Acts 8:1b, 4

Persecution scattered the church out of its birthplace of Jerusalem into the surrounding regions of Israel. Because of that scattering, the proclamation of the gospel happened in new places for those who needed to hear. This was God's doing. Suffering was a significant component in getting the good news of Jesus out there.

The zealous persecutor of the church, Saul, encountered the resurrected Christ on the road to Damascus. Being temporarily blinded, God sent Ananias to restore his sight. Even more, he had a message for Saul from God. The Lord stated it to Ananias this way:

Go, for he is a chosen instrument of mine to carry my name before the Gentiles and kings and the children of Israel. For I will show him how much he must suffer for the sake of my name. Acts 9:15-16.

Suffering is closely connected with the progress of the gospel. We don't appreciate that message, but it is true. Of the many places I have traveled, I have seen the church most obedient, vibrant and fruitful where believers are suffering for the sake of Christ. In fact, I would say that the church's health and fruitfulness is directly proportional to the amount it is suffering. Why?

Since therefore Christ suffered in the flesh, arm yourselves with the same way of thinking, for whoever has suffered in the flesh has ceased from sin, so as to live for the rest of the time in the flesh no longer for human passions but for the will of God. 1Peter 4:1-2

Beloved, do not be surprised at the fiery trial when it comes upon you to test you, as though something strange were happening to you. But rejoice insofar as you share Christ's sufferings, that you may also rejoice and be glad when his glory is revealed. (1Peter 4:12-13)

» Suffering draws a line in the sand. You are either a committed Christ follower or you are not one at all.

» Suffering cleanses believers from the sins that so easily entangle us.

» Suffering removes self-promoting agendas along with the pursuit of ease or comfort.

» Suffering binds us to Christ since he has also called us to suffer.

2 Corinthians 11:16-33

I repeat, let no one think me foolish. But even if you do, accept me as a fool, so that I too may boast a little. What I am saying with this boastful confidence, I say not as the Lord would but as a fool. Since many boast according to the flesh, I too will boast. For you gladly bear with fools, being wise yourselves! For you bear it if someone makes slaves of you, or devours you, or takes advantage of you, or puts on airs, or strikes you in the face. To my shame, I must say, we were too weak for that!

But whatever anyone else dares to boast of—I am speaking as a fool—I also dare to boast of that. Are they Hebrews? So am I. Are they Israelites? So am I. Are they offspring of Abraham? So am I. Are they servants of Christ? I am a better one—I am talking like a madman—with far greater labors, far more imprisonments, with countless beatings, and often near death. Five times I received at the hands of the Jews the forty lashes less one. Three times I was beaten with rods. Once I was stoned. Three times I was shipwrecked; a night and a day I was adrift at sea; on frequent journeys, in danger from rivers, danger from robbers, danger from my own people, danger from Gentiles, danger in the city, danger in the wilderness, danger at sea, danger from false brothers; in toil and hardship, through many a sleepless night, in hunger and thirst, often without food, in cold and exposure. And, apart from other things, there is the daily pressure on me of my anxiety for all the churches. Who is weak, and I am not weak? Who is made to fall, and I am not indignant?

If I must boast, I will boast of the things that show my weakness. The God and Father of the Lord Jesus, he who is blessed forever, knows that I am not lying. At Damascus, the governor under King Aretas was guarding the city of Damascus in order to seize me, but I was let down in a basket through a window in the wall and escaped his hands.

The question Westerners need to ask is this: If I am not suffering for the gospel, am I risking enough for Christ's sake? Maybe we live in a place and time where suffering is not a part of the discipleship process. Or maybe we have settled to risk nothing.

The great apostle Paul laid everything on the line. He suffered for it, too. If you want to be reminded of Paul's sacrifices for the sake of Christ, read 2Corinthians 11:16-33. Nearing the end of his life, Paul stated how he felt about all of this:

For I will not venture to speak of anything except what Christ has accomplished through me to bring the Gentiles to obedience—by word and deed, 19 by the power of signs and wonders, by the power of the Spirit of God—so that from Jerusalem and all the way around to Illyricum I have fulfilled the ministry of the gospel of Christ. Romans 15:18-19

As for the signs and wonders Paul mentions–also described throughout the book of Acts and anticipated in the New Testament letters–we still see them in abundance making significant inroads to unreached peoples all around the world today. Among Hindu people, we often see miracles of healing. It enables them to see that among their millions of gods, none can do what Jesus can do. With Muslim peoples, visions and signs are often the tipping point in leading them to Christ. God is still passionate to do whatever it takes to help people know him. He simply needs people of radical risk-taking faith who will lay everything on the line for the glory of Christ.

STRATEGIES OF MULTIPLICATION

Jesus modeled multiplication as he developed his disciples. They carried on this methodology. Addition is not bad. It brings people into the kingdom. Multiplication always begins with addition but reaches a systematic reproductive dynamic. It is better, always leading to much greater and more sustainable long-term results.

» Addition focuses on finding followers, multiplication develops reproducers.

» Addition births disciples, multiplication develops disciple-makers who develop disciple-makers.

» Addition generally focuses on a crowd, multiplication deeply focuses on a few.

» Addition is often more impressive early on, multiplication often starts small and inconspicuous.

» Addition appeals to those wanting quick measurable results, multiplication takes faith, perseverance and hope.

» Addition will make an impact, multiplication will bring transformation to entire regions for the sake of Christ.

Movements always involve strategies of multiplication that are empowered by the Holy Spirit. They take on a life of their own! Consider reading Acts 19--it reveals the following dynamics of a gospel movement:

1. A rapid spread of the gospel. People cannot help but tell others who need to know the good news of Jesus Christ.

2. Lives transformed. The most unlikely people will come to faith in Christ and become champions of spreading the gospel to others.

3. Communities impacted. Sinful cultural realities are challenged, religious systems are upset and the opportunity for a new way of living cannot be overlooked.

4. Churches started. When believers embrace Christ, they will also develop communities of Christ-followers in which to learn, develop, be encouraged and find strength to persevere.

One added item: Almost always, along with the above movement dynamics, will be suffering and persecution experienced by those involved.

Here's a quick review of the primary dynamics present within the early church:

1   Selfless generosity was a significant factor in how influential the church became.

2   Suffering, signs and wonders were the means of making inroads to unreached people and regions.

3   Strategies of true multiplication enabled the church to see crucial movements take place.

I hope you are reminded of how relevant and radical the church is meant to be. All the above realities were experienced only as the church was courageously and sacrificially engaged in obeying the great commission--to make disciples of all nations no matter the cost. This is a sobering and humbling reminder of what it means to be the church. What will you do with this?

"God is still passionate to do whatever it takes to help people know him. He simply needs people of radical risk-taking faith who will lay everything on the line for the glory of Christ."

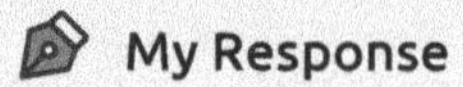 My Response

PERSONAL REFLECTION:

Which of the three dynamics present in the early church challenge you the most and why?

OBSERVATION:

Which of the early church characteristics seems to be most improbable today? Why do you think this?

Every church has room to grow into God's heart for the world

I've put together a handful of resources that I think will challenge you and your church. God has a big vision for the world; we need a big vision too.

faroffsaints.com/early-church

ACTION STEP:

Write a simple prayer expressing what you are feeling right now.

Early Church Priorities

But you will receive power when the Holy Spirit has come upon you, and you will be my witnesses in Jerusalem and in all Judea and Samaria, and to the end of the earth. Acts 1:8

The above verse is most probably the last of several commissions Jesus gave to His disciples over a period of forty days following the resurrection, from Galilee to the Mount of Olives where he ascended to the Father. Each one states the same desired outcome (that the whole world would know about salvation through Christ), but with various nuances emphasizing the various ways this command should be carried out. The Acts 1 commission emphasizes two things:

1   The role of the Holy Spirit in being Christ's witnesses (We will reflect briefly on this.)

2   The four dimensions of ministry his followers were to intentionally engage in. (This will be our primary consideration for today.)

A witness is someone who tells what they know about something. There are two types of witnesses in a courtroom, for example:

1   A material witness simply tells what they have seen, heard or experienced. They tell their story related to the person or case at hand.

They do not need to be specialists in any way. The material witness speaks from their human experience. Jesus calls ALL believers to be this—to tell what they have seen, heard and experienced.

2. An expert witness is someone with specialized knowledge or ability. I have a friend who is a forensic psychologist who is often called to testify in courtrooms about the mental state and most likely scenarios that lend weight to the jury's considerations of a case. He's seen it all! And very few people can provide what he does since he is highly educated, gifted and experienced in these matters. The expert witnesses in the church are the approximate 10% of believers who have the spiritual gift of evangelism. They can speak into the evangelism process better than most since they're the experts. By the way, they need the Holy Spirit to empower them, too.

Whether a material or expert witness, the Holy Spirit has been given to you to help you succeed in this witnessing role. He does this by...

>> Helping you see those around you who need Jesus.

>> Helping you know how God is at work in someone's life at any given moment.

>> Preparing the mind and softening the heart of the person who needs Christ.

>> Bringing the right thoughts and words to mind as you need them.

>> Giving you courage and boldness as needed--patience and grace as needed, too.

>> Empowering you to take risks, perform miracles or anything else you need God's help with.

>> Performing the miraculous transformation from death to life that only He can do.

If we try to be witnesses for Christ without the Holy Spirit's power, it becomes a limited disappointing experience for all involved. And besides, why try without this amazing gift God has given to every believer in Christ?! The Holy Spirit's involvement in witnessing to others is our only hope for success in this great endeavor.

This witnessing activity is to take place in four primary dimensions of life and ministry—Jerusalem, Judea, Samaria and to the end of the earth. At least this is how it was stated to those present with Jesus at the time. What does this mean for us today?

Jerusalem was where they were. Ground zero. It's where the church would be planted in about a week after Jesus' ascension. They needed to be witnesses of Jesus here for sure! God had them here for a reason. The people in Jerusalem, though they knew more about this gospel story than any other place at this time, still needed to hear testimonies about the person and power of Jesus. They still didn't "get it", but they needed to.

Every local church is planted where it is to be a witness for Christ. You are in your neighborhood, apartment, or dorm to be salt and light where you are. This is why you are where you are. You may be the best opportunity those around you have of ever coming to know Jesus. This is your Jerusalem.

Judea was the region around Jerusalem. Jesus was being quite specific in this statement—don't only reach the city where you live but to influence those outside your place of daily activities. This means that we need to constantly think of how our impact for Christ can expand. We should never settle. Others outside our direct sphere of influence need Jesus, too.

Our American churches are getting creative about how to expand their influence. I love that! Push out! Be creative! Be risky! Be bold! And don't do it to chalk up numbers or have bragging rights. Do it so lost people can be transformed by Jesus.

Samaria was the big challenge for those first hearers. Samaritans were deeply despised by most Jews at the time. They were considered half-breeds, traitors and the worst of the worst. These were the people few Israelites ever thought of having a relationship with. People didn't do that with them. But Jesus tells his followers to break down the barriers, see them as precious, press through their prejudices, take risks, love the unlovely as Jesus loved them and step into their world in obedience to Christ. History didn't matter. Their belief system didn't matter. Their differences didn't matter. "Just do it!" Jesus said. "Be my witnesses there!"

Who is our Samaria? It's different for each of us. Most likely, it is that cross-cultural group you rarely think of engaging with. It may be those people you don't really see—you just look past them. You may think it's futile to engage—that nothing good would ever come from that. Or it's too risky or uncomfortable. Or you wouldn't know what to say or how to say it. Or what if they hated you or laughed or thought you were crazy or even hurt you. Believe me, the list is endless of why we shouldn't engage our Samarias, but there is one good reason we should. Jesus told us to.

God is doing a new thing in our time: He is bringing the peoples of the world to our neighborhoods. Do you believe God directs the affairs of mankind? Well, he's directing people from far away into our backyards, across the street and into our places of work. Why? These Samaritans need to meet Jesus. We dare not ignore what God is doing in these days. The churches and individuals that respond to this great movement will find the favor of God in their lives. Obedience has beautiful results.

"The end of the earth", in the Greek language, most literally means last or least valued of the world. While we often talk about the second coming of Jesus, millions in the world have never heard of His first coming. The greatest injustice in the world is for a person to be born, live and die never having heard a credible presentation of the gospel. That injustice happens to over 70,000 people who die every day among the unreached peoples of the world. They have been overlooked and undervalued. They are last—the ends of the earth.

This is not a simple task. It requires sacrifice, perseverance, faith, patience and consistent intentionality. But it is the task of the church. It has been since the time of Jesus to this day. We cannot relent. This is what Jesus told his fol-lowers to be about. We do this by:

>> Praying

>> Sending

>> Supporting

>> Engaging when possible

>> Resourcing

I could say so much about each of the above activities. For now, let's simply realize that this global task is ours by command of Christ.

Let's make one more observation from Acts 1:8. Each of the four dimensions of ministry are connected with the conjunction "and". The sentence holds a rare grammatical structure in the Greek language by having all these conjunctions one after another. Why? Because this four-fold ministry is to happen simultaneously in the church, not sequentially.

>> We should not wait until we reach our Jerusalem to engage our Judea.

>> We should not wait until we reach our Judea to engage our Samaria.

>> We should not wait until we reach our Samaria to engage the ends of the earth.

These four dimensions should all happen simultaneously in every local church as God specifically directs. Though I have often heard, "We need to get our act together here before we do something there", this is not God's way. Maybe that is why there are still 7,000 unreached people groups left in the world. Maybe too many of us leading our churches are waiting to get our act together at home before we start intentionally engaging those far away. But maybe–just maybe–the way to get our act together is to simply do what Jesus has told us to do here, near *and* far off.

 My Response

PERSONAL REFLECTION:

In which of the four dimensions of ministry is your church strongest? How about the weakest?

OBSERVATION:

How are you personally challenged by Acts 1:8?

Every church has room to grow into God's heart for the world

I've put together a handful of resources that I think will challenge you and your church. God has a big vision for the world; we need a big vision too.

faroffsaints.com/priorities

ACTION STEP:

What next step could you take to make progress in obeying Jesus' command here?

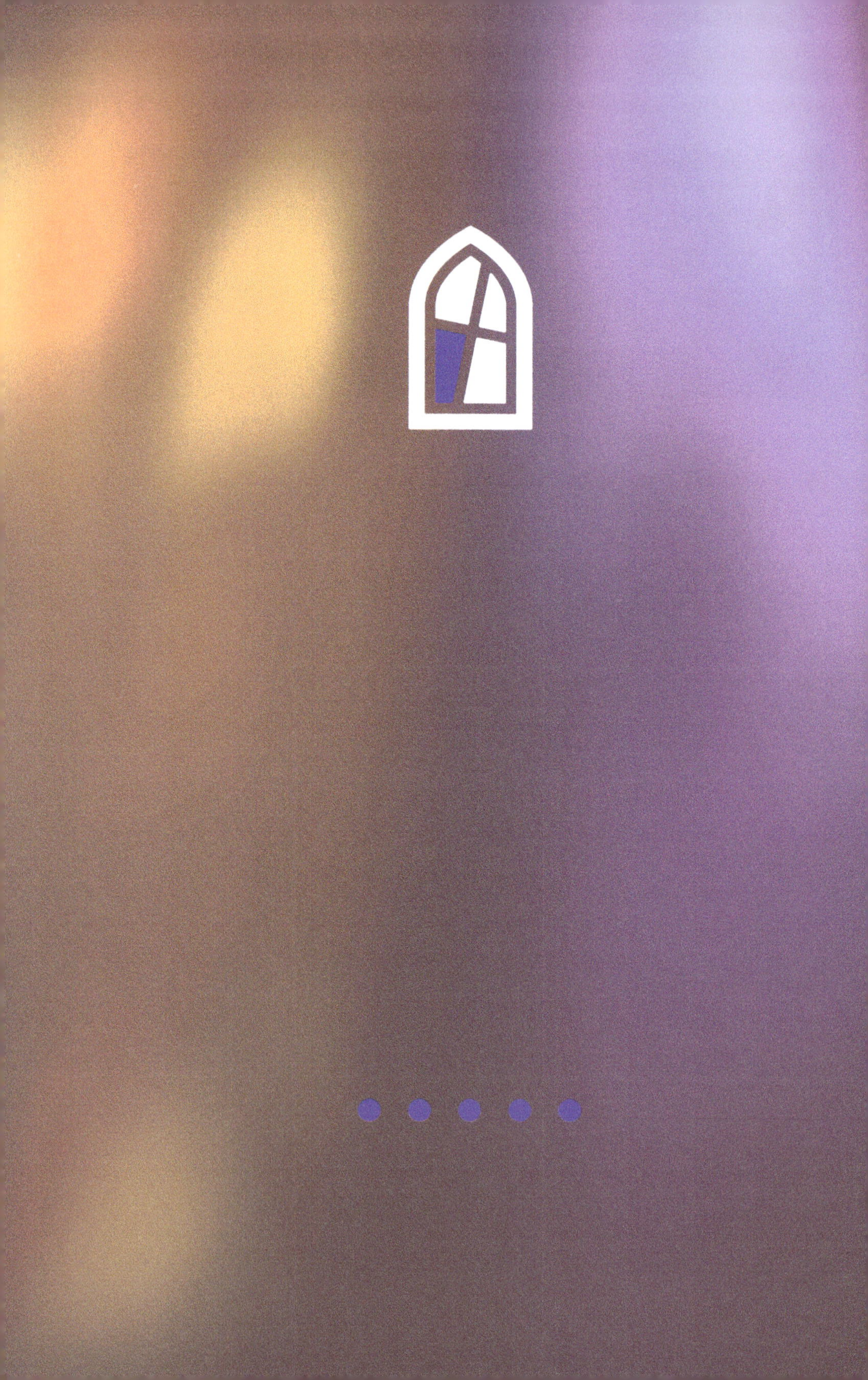

The Church's Unfinished Task

In a city of over 100,000 people, this was the only church. The urban center was teaming with a robust economy, steeped in a respected history and carnal to the core. So many here had embraced a religion that appealed to the basest drives of human nature, promoting free sexuality and orgies as part of their acceptable lifestyles. Wealth was rampant, false religion flourished, the economy was booming and life was good. Most people didn't think twice about attending church or becoming part of this new and strange community of Jesus followers. Still, the church stood out like a candle on a lampstand in a very dark place. The light penetrated the darkness and the church became robust as it developed disciples to resist the raging currents of the culture's influence.

This new church was no fly by night happenstance, either. The very best of church planters helped start it by laying a spiritually strong foundation, identifying leaders, teaching them deeply, networking them with other churches nearby and routinely checking in to assure they were doing OK. There were new and thriving churches 30 miles to the northwest and 45 miles west. Another within 10 miles to the east. The Holy Spirit was at work in and through this church as radical transformations took place, even miracles that brought many more to faith in Jesus. Everything was working.

Forty-five years later, the church was on the brink of collapse. This once vibrant church was now experiencing spiritual deadness to the core. No one wanted to identify it or face it or say it. Most knew there was something missing, but all continued to put on a façade of happiness and health. Sin went unchecked while most had adapted to the tantalizing culture, incorporating the practices of their city into their form of religion. They had become masters at rationalizing sin, over-emphasizing God's grace, and overlooking the real purpose for which this church was planted. There were a few stalwart believers still hanging on, crying out to God and maintaining their unsoiled commitment to Jesus. But only a few.

That church eventually did die. God's favor was withdrawn and the church crumbled, another church lifespan concluded before its time.

By the way, this church was planted by the Apostle Paul (maybe the best church planter in history) in the city of Sardis (in current-day Turkey) around the year 50AD. 45 years later, in the midst of the Sardis church collapse, the Apostle John wrote to them on behalf of Jesus:

> *I know your deeds; you have a reputation of being alive, but you are dead. Wake up! Strengthen what remains and is about to die, for I have found your deeds unfinished in the sight of my God.*
>
> *Remember, therefore, what you have received and heard; hold it fast, and repent. But if you do not wake up, I will come like a thief, and you will not know at what time I will come to you.*
>
> *Yet you have a few people in Sardis who have not soiled their clothes. They will walk with me, dressed in white, for they are worthy.*
>
> *Revelation 3:1b-4*

I often think of the seven churches of Revelation. Where are they now? Even the best of them have faded into oblivion. What does this mean? It means that the church is imperfect, and that each local congregation is a living organism with a lifespan and season to obediently follow hard after God. I hope I'm not being too pessimistic, but the church does not automatically receive the favor and blessing of God. We do not naturally produce fruit or make disciples or become vibrant or step into God's best plan for expanding ministry. Every church in every season and every location needs to be sold out to the purposes and plans of God. If we're not, though God still loves us and provides salvation for us, we will not be obedient vital players in God's global agenda. This applies to us as individuals, as well.

STRENGTHEN WHAT REMAINS AND FINISH THE TASK

The Words to the churches of Revelation are penetrating, straight forward, sobering, and true. What would Jesus' letter to our church state today? For Sardis, we see a couple of powerful phrases in Revelation 3:2 that I would like us to ponder a bit:

1 "Strengthen What Remains"

This phrase tells us that the Sardis church is weakened (not as strong as it was) and it has lost some things (only some remains are left). Every church starts with strength in the areas of its mission, passion and resolve. A clear purpose drives a handful of believers to sacrifice and work diligently to see a new church born. An ambivalent unfocused church planting core will never see a promising church birthed. Inevitably, however, fatigue sets in, focus wanes, commitment eases, sacrifice lessens, and clarity gets foggy. The only way a church can press on to have the influence God intends is through consistent recurring sober assessment, realignment to the church's founding purpose and recommitments to be sacrificial and holy. Sardis had lost much of its founding pizazz and began to drift into modes of maintenance and mediocrity. This did not please the Lord as we have his declared warning of impending doom if things didn't change:

Remember, therefore, what you have received and heard; hold it fast, and repent. But if you do not wake up, I will come like a thief, and you will not know at what time I will come to you. Revelation 3:3

2 "Finish the Task"

Jesus stated to the Sardis church that he found "their deeds unfinished." It's no secret that the image of a lamp stand was used to symbolize each of the seven churches mentioned in Revelation 2 and 3. That's because the ultimate purpose of the church was to be a light in the darkness. The "deed" expected above everything else was to bring light in the darkness and make disciples of all nations. Evidently, the influence of this church was "unfinished". Its resolve has wavered, clarity of mission was foggy, passion for holiness had died (except for a few) and impact stunted. We don't know for sure, but if church history and church dynamics tell us anything, they may have become a little like the lifesaving station we read about at the beginning of the week. Our presence has become more about us—our hopes, dreams and agenda--rather than that of saving lives no matter the cost.

As I consider Christ's church in these days, I sometimes wonder if:

» We have wanted to grow our own congregations more than God's Kingdom

» We have valued cultural relevance more than spiritual relevance

» We have pursued bragging rights more than being bragged on by Christ

» We have developed a spirituality in our heads more than in our actions

» We have adopted an out-of-sight out-of-mind approach to global ministry

» We have too easily cast aside meaningful missions because it's hard

» We have been selfish with our people, money and resources

>> We have not prayed strategically

>> We have not acted courageously

>> We have not lived sacrificially

If we can learn anything from Scripture about the church, anything from history about what can happen, let's be bold in assessing our true passion and alignment with God's objectives for his church. The truth is our friend—because none is so blind as they who choose not to see the truth.

THE CHURCH IN THE MISSION OF GOD

Throughout history, the church looks and functions differently since it exists within its culture. This is one of the beautiful characteristics of a biblical church. God, in his paramount wisdom, knew that a cookie-cutter church model would not work in a world made up of variety, creativity and contrasts. People of every culture express themselves differently, process information uniquely, have felt needs peculiar to them and have their own special dynamics of interrelating with one another. The church around the world is as unique and diverse as the people and cultures in which they reside.

Ecclesiology is the theology and study of the church. We cannot begin to address the depths and complexities of the church in a couple paragraphs. Though volumes have been written on the purpose, nature and function of the church, I do need to succinctly state a few clarifications for our purposes here.

>> The church is always called to be biblical. It must understand the nature, purpose and function of its existence and continually pursue a culturally appropriate church that is uncompromisingly biblical.

>> The church will always have the same primary mission. Needs and uniqueness of each setting require the church to respond in ways that make her relevant, but the core purpose is always the same.

>> The church often becomes less than God intended. Sin, the human condition and culture always tantalizes the church to drift from its purpose and effectiveness.

Attempting to be as biblical and simple as possible, the organization I lead describes its mission of "starting and strengthening churches worldwide" in the following way:

We are committed to developing communities of Jesus followers who regularly meet and fellowship in reproducing multiplying movements that holistically impact individuals, communities and regions through the power of the gospel.

It's biblical, simple, adaptable for all cultures and driven by the mission of God for the sake of all far off saints.

"*Every church in every season and every location needs to be sold out to the purposes and plans of God. If we're not, though God still loves us and provides salvation for us, we will not be obedient vital players in God's global agenda.*"

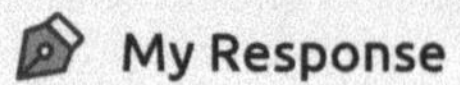 My Response

PERSONAL REFLECTION:

What thoughts do you have about "church drift" after today's reading?

OBSERVATION:

In what way is your church spot on in God's mission? Where does it need a little work?

Every church has room to grow into God's heart for the world

I've put together a handful of resources that I think will challenge you and your church. God has a big vision for the world; we need a big vision too.

faroffsaints.com/unfinished

ACTION STEP:

Write a short prayer for your church in light of Jesus' words to Sardis and what you've been challenged with this week.

WEEK THREE TAKE AWAY:

Of all you read and experienced in Far Off Saints this week, what one truth will you embrace or action you will take?

SMALL GROUP MATERIALS

Could the Church be Far Off?

GETTING STARTED: (10 MINUTES)

Spend a little time mingling and catching up with your Far Off Saints group members.

Begin with Prayer, dedicating these remaining two weeks of Far Off Saints to the Lord. Ask him to meet you powerfully as you engage in his Word and with one another today.

BREAKING THE ICE: (10 MINUTES)

From our Far Off Saints readings so far in week three, what has captured your attention or challenged you significantly? Explain if possible.

VIDEO TEACHING: (30 MINUTES)

» Watch #3 – <u>City On a Hill</u>

» What spoke to you most from today's teaching?

» Follow up Question: In what ways do you think today's church at large is engaging effectively in God's global plan of redemption? How is it falling short?

SCRIPTURE STUDY: (25 MINUTES)

Read Acts 4:32-37

» What qualities and activities characterized this Jerusalem church? Go ahead and make a list.

» Does this sound like a perfect church? Why or why not?

» How do you think the events earlier in chapter 4 shaped them as a church?

How do you think this church became...

» Unified?

» Evangelistic?

» Selfless and generous?

» Is there anything that ties all of these outstanding characteristics together?

» If we as individuals—and then as a church—became more like this, what might happen in our community? What might happen with our global influence?

» As God's people who make up Christ's church here and now, what first steps could we take to move toward this, being certain we are not "far off"?

CONCLUSION: (15 MINUTES)

What is your take-away from this evening? (That is, what is your next step with what you've heard and experienced?)

Close in group prayer, with opportunities for all to pray, asking God to work in and through your church in fresh new ways. Be sure to pray for your pastor and the leaders of your congregation, giving thanks to God for them.

How Can I Not Be Far Off?

Far off in Nepal, a dozen of us Americans traveled to participate and help lead a gathering of 1100 Nepali church planters. This was truly incredible since only 50 years earlier, there were only 40 known believers in the entire country. Now a massive crowd of future church planters gathered in Kathmandu to learn about starting new churches, set goals for their nation, and be encouraged to get it done. Susan and I were privileged to be here with the U.S. organization that fueled this gathering.

Of the many things that happened in those few days, the foot washing has been indelibly etched into my memory. It's unfortunate that Americans are often seen as superior. In cross-cultural settings, we are always honored, esteemed by those who sit in rapped attention at our every word. We get the seats of honor, the heads of the table, the best foods and always the podiums from which to speak. Many people in least-reached areas believe that if they could only be like the American Christians, they would have arrived. Just know that this fallacy doesn't serve the global church well. We need so many qualities that the global church has acquired so well. Our team understood this clearly. In no way did we want the Nepali believers and church planters to suppose that they were serving us. We had come to serve them! So we decided to wash their feet to make the point.

On one afternoon, about 50 Nepali leaders of regions and people groups gathered for a special time of encouragement and challenge. Our plan, however, was to wash their feet in Jesus' name. After everyone was present for this special meeting, we explained what we foreigners were going to do. There was concern on some of their faces, shock on others, and a sense of disbelief among still more. With the wash basins and towels ready, our small group of white visitors began washing the feet of the Nepali church leaders. The Holy Spirit fell on us.

I remember dirty feet. Really dirty feet that had traveled miles upon miles in sandals having scaled mountains and trekked through valleys to get here. I remember weeping. Weeping by the Nepalis being washed and weeping by the Americans washing them. I remember fervent prayers in Jesus' name that the Holy Spirit would empower these courageous and sold-out believers to plant churches in hard places at the risk of their lives and freedom. I remember brothers and sisters in Christ laying their heads on one another's shoulders as they wept like babies. I remember these locals trying to say in broken English, "Thank you" and "God bless you" as tears streamed down their faces.

We weren't fully serving in the way Jesus intended by taking on the weaker position, getting down and dirty with the Nepali people and sacrificing in the spirit of Jesus. We simply washed feet. We got on our knees for an hour in a symbolic act to elevate the value and importance of the Nepali pastors. But even with that, the symbolism was powerful, reminding us once again that being a disciple is all about serving others here, near and far off.

Jesus said, "If I then, your Lord and Teacher, have washed your feet, you also ought to wash one another's feet," John 13:14.

The Apostle Paul later wrote, "Do nothing from selfish ambition or conceit, but in humility count others more significant than yourselves," Philippians 2:3.

Jesus, the missionary God, taught us that our mission is to serve others. The great task of global disciplemaking stands before us. It requires sold out servants to get it done.

» The task will not be done by worldly people.

» The task will not get done by half-hearted or nicely religious people.

» The task will not get done by a carnal, misdirected, or well-intentioned Church.

» The task will not get done by human ingenuity or determination.

» **The task will be completed by sold out servants** who are humble, sacrificial, and faithful.

The task can get done without you. God tells us in His word that the fulfillment of this task will happen. The church will accomplish the task entrusted to her. The task can get done without you, but is that what you really want?

We are to resemble the apostle Paul when he stated, "But one thing I do, forgetting what lies behind and straining forward to what lies ahead, I press on toward the goal for the prize of the upward call of God in Christ Jesus," Philippians 3:13-14. Can we be sure God wants us to have this same attitude? Yes! Because the following verse clarifies, "Let those of us who are mature think this way, and if in anything you think otherwise, God will reveal that also to you," Philippians 3:15.

In the last week of these studies, we will come to better understand what each of our roles may be and how we can courageously step into it. We will be challenged to become humble foot-washing servants on a mission here, near and far off.

Acquire God's Heart for Lost People

The Cook Islands are way out there! Far from anywhere, these remote South Pacific Islands were a landing pad for me while traveling to some hard-to-get-to places in the mid 1990s. With four days layover being the only way for me to get to my next destination, I hunkered down in a pretty nice place in this beautiful tropical paradise.

And then I "accidentally" met Richard, an American in his twenties living alone on the island. As we struck up conversation on my first day there, we soon realized we had many things in common. Paramount in our connection was a mutual love for Jesus. He invited me to his house later that night for his home-made chili.

When Richard arrived late that afternoon, I saw that a moped ride was in my near future. That was his only mode of transportation beside his legs. I wondered what the rest of the evening would hold for me, wondering afresh if this guy was the real deal. I didn't know if he would mug me, drug me, or who knows what. I must admit, I started to question whether I had trusted some-one too soon and had made a foolish decision. We soon arrived at his home on the beach—a 12-foot by 12-foot tin hut shadowed by coconut palms and surrounded by various coastal shrubs. It was a beach house with an amazing ocean-front view! This was outstanding! And I began to relax as he invited me in to view his simple home. The luscious aroma of simmering chili filled the air, mixed with the salty breeze of the Pacific. It was heavenly.

The evening was unforgettable as we sat outside his front door chowing down chili and cornbread and having great conversations as we told our stories. Here's what I learned about Richard:

>> He was a homeless person in the U.S. for some time, even describing the bridge he lived beneath in my home city for a season. I knew exactly where that was.

>> He came to know Jesus because someone cared enough to share the gospel with him.

>> He connected to Youth with a Mission (YWAM) and went to their School for the Nations where he quickly learned Scripture and biblical principles of discipleship and ministry.

>> He was sent to Rarotonga, Cook Islands with a YWAM team and served with them for two or three years. YWAM decided they needed to pull out of the Cook Islands, but Richard had knitted his heart to the people and needs of this tiny Pacific nation, deciding to stay solo.

>> He lived on 150 dollars a month from a few friends who sent him donations regularly.

>> He committed to help raise up a generation of children to be the Christian leaders of the future for the Cook Islands. He did this through a small school and various other creative means.

>> He started a Christian radio station on the island and even solicited some U.S. broadcasts from organizations like Focus on the Family and Chuck Swindoll.

Quite frankly, I was blown away by his resolve, love for lost people, innovation, and pioneering spirit to accomplish his calling. Beach-side and all, I was stunned by the simple sacrificial way he lived his life every day. I was humbled by this young man who was serving Jesus faithfully though few others in the world knew or would ever notice. The lost people and the societal needs of this remote nation had gripped Richard's heart. He acted on it in decisive and intentional ways.

Most of us will never be a Richard. This is not God's call on most of our lives. But we still need to know God's heart for lost people. God has expressed His love, compassion, and determination to bring new life to people caught in sin and death. "For God so loved the world that He gave His only begotten son that whosoever believes in Him will not perish, but have everlasting life," John 3:16. Always remember, our God is a missionary God. He spanned the distance between us and God, between Heaven and earth to redeem us, paying a sin-debt that only He could pay. He has accomplished the unimaginable for completely sinful people out of an infinite love that meets us where we are.

>> And if we truly love God, we will love who He loves.

>> If we are followers of Jesus, we will value who He values.

Jesus himself said, "If you love me, you will keep my commandments." One of the most important commands was the last one entrusted to us, "Go and make disciples of all nations." If we flippantly disregard this or choose to be busy with other things that supposedly matter—or decide we will "get there" at some point--we are not loving God properly. Love is not a feeling, but action in alignment with the desires and benefits of the One you are loving. God's expectation—and one of the critical ways we love him—is that each of us become a part of his larger plan for our fallen world.

HOW DO WE ACQUIRE GOD'S HEART FOR LOST PEOPLE?

1 Don't try harder. Train better.

In Luke 15, Jesus told a couple parables about lost things—a lost sheep and a lost coin. After reflecting on these passages, the first inclination is to try harder at noticing and finding those who are lost. But if you ponder those parables for a moment, there is a simple and profound truth that applies here. No one needed to tell the shepherd to search for the lost sheep. He so loved the lost sheep that nothing could hold him back from finding it. He was driven to find the lost one. And so it is with the woman and the lost coin. She had such a desire to find the missing coin that she rummaged through her entire home to find it. No one forced her to find it. The value of the coin drove her to action. There was no trying involved.

This brings us to the core of engaging with God in the great task before us. If it is not in our heart, no amount of trying will get us there. Instead, we must train well. Training well involves several disciplines that shape your heart to be like God's heart. When our heart is in alignment with God's, we will be driven to pursue the things that God pursues. We will love the lost, have compassion for the needy, seek healing for the broken and salvation for sinners. It may sound a little idealistic, but this is the way God intends it to be. Even the disciples could not accomplish their roles without the filling of the Holy Spirit in their lives, that is, God living in and through them. And that's what we need more than anything.

What are some of the training activities we need to engage in? Let me provide a cursory list:

2   Find Your Focus.

Did you know your focus becomes your reality? Have you ever gone into a store, saw something you really liked and decided you needed it? That's why it's always dangerous for me to go to a car lot. I may suddenly think I need something there that I haven't even thought of before. Your focus does become your reality and in much more significant ways than what you see in a store or a used car lot.

Jesus said to Peter, "Do you love me more than these?" John 21:15. The "these" in this verse is most likely the fish he kept going back to. Jesus wasn't trying to have a "love competition" between Peter and the other disciples.

They were not the "these". Peter loved fish and fishing. That's what he kept going back to—his default way of living life. Jesus was saying, "Peter, you need to change your focus. This isn't what matters anymore. If you love me, then make me your focus, not these fish."

What's your focus? What consumes you, your time, energy, resources, expenses? What do you keep going back to? What are you driven to do, participate in, and lose time and energy doing? Is it your job, fun, material things, a bigger paycheck, building your retirement funds or savings accounts, your smartphone, politics, conspiracy theories, social media, television, or music?

And Jesus gently says, "Do you love me more than these?" John 21:15.

Finding your focus requires you to decide who you're going to serve: Yourself or God? It's simple and it's big. Will you live for yourself, your agenda, your pleasures and wants? Or will you live for God, his agenda, his pleasure and his plan? Your focus becomes your reality. What you focus on fills your heart. As Solomon stated, "Guard your heart with all diligence for from it flow the springs of life." Proverbs 4:23.

Let me suggest a few action steps on this one:

» Listen closely for God's heart to be revealed to you.

» Read the Word seeking to hear truth. (This study has been a good start.)

» Find some good books that will stir your heart for God-things. (I have some suggestions at the end.)

» Listen to some messages or podcasts that speak of God's heart for the world.

» Pursue this important discipline of knowing God's heart in every way you can.

» Ask a missionary why they are a missionary. Dig a little. If you need help finding a global worker to talk with, we would love to help you get connected. Go to www.faroffsaints.com/connect

3   Pray for lost people here, near and far. Part of the value of praying is that it changes us. As we invest in praying for lost people, God instills a passion for these people in our hearts. God hears those prayers, too. I have seen revival happen in churches because people began consistently and faithfully praying for lost people. It transformed the lives of lost people—and the believers who prayed for them.

Write the names of people down that you are praying for, the unreached people group(s) that you're praying for and the "Samaritans" in your area you're praying for. Then, faithfully and consistently pray until something miraculous happens. I dare you.

4   Go on a mission trip, if possible, to some least-reached people. I promise you, you'll never be the same. Every mission trip changes you somehow, but when you go to see and serve people who have never heard of Jesus—Wow! It does something to your heart. Do that!

5   Remember what it's like to be lost. Something strange happens to us once we've been a believer for a while. We forget what it's like to be lost. Unless you became a Christ-follower as a child, I challenge you to take an evening to ponder your earlier lost condition. Feel again what it was like to be hopeless, confused, without answers, feeling dead inside and so on. Let it saturate you. Then pray to have the eyes and compassion of Christ as you go about your life in the place God has put you. You are there to be salt and light, but it's way too easy to lose our effectiveness when we've forgotten what it's like to be lost.

"Your focus becomes your reality. What you focus on fills your heart. As Solomon stated, 'Guard your heart with all diligence for from it flow the springs of life.'"

PERSONAL REFLECTIONS:

What challenges you the most in today's reading and why?

OBSERVATION:

On a scale of one to ten, how do you rate "your heart for lost people?"

1 2 3 4 5 6 7 8 9 10

Are you moving on the scale to the right or to the left?

Resource suggestions to acquire God's heart for lost people

I've collected a variety resources to help you dive deeper into learning about God's passion for all people. Dive in to one or two of these!

faroffsaints.com/gods-heart

ACTION STEP:

There are five suggestions listed in acquiring God's heart for lost people. Which one will you engage with and what's your first step to get that to happen?

Become a Global Christian

The more I engage with the world's peoples and cultures, the richer I become.

My first mission trip happened when I was 35 years old. It changed my life. The Billy Graham Association sent me to Vorkuta, Russia to oversee a satellite crusade in this city of 500,000 secluded from the rest of the world. In 1993, this city on the edge of Siberia was still reeling from the dark days of Stalin where millions of political prisoners were sentenced and died in the twelve coal mines that surrounded the city. One local stated what everyone believed: "The railroad tracks were built on the bones of dead men."

The church was just emerging from an underground existence—communism had recently fallen. Gripped by fear, shaped by generations of oppression, the church was risking outreach for the first time in centuries. As for me, I was so honored to represent Billy Graham to these people, but severely humbled by the perseverance and resilience of these formidable Russian believers. I saw what real faith looked like, recognized my privileged position in the world, understood the depth of darkness among hopeless people and vowed to bring the gospel to those without access to the truths of Jesus Christ.

Since then, I have worked and served in over sixty countries and experienced unfathomable lostness among people who still have never heard of

Jesus. My heart was both broken and made alive in Russia. Knowledge in my head became conviction in my heart. This calling has continued to drive me to this day.

Ignorance is not bliss when it comes to global awareness. When we have a world-view that is only Western, we live our lives with a fraction of the understanding God intends for us. When our ministry and mission encompass only our congregations or communities, we have overlooked God's passionate heart for the lost peoples of the world. Without becoming a global Christian, we risk the high probability that we will engage in the sin of omission. The out-of-sight out-of-mind philosophy may work to assuage our conscience, but it will never suffice for holiness before God.

WHAT CAN YOU DO TO BECOME A GLOBAL CHRISTIAN?

1   Read Scripture with fresh eyes and a hungry heart. We see what we're looking for.

Have you had the experience of purchasing a new vehicle and suddenly seeing this vehicle everywhere? You didn't see it before, but you sure do now. It's because you see what you're looking for. Hopefully, through these readings, you've become more aware of God's heart for lost people, his plan for our broken world and our part in that plan. Now, open your Bibles and read with fresh eyes for those new things God wants to show you. I encourage you to have a notebook and pen in hand to jot down the fresh insights God is eager to give you. When you find something new, share it with someone you trust. When God's truths get in you and through you, they really stick. It will help you become a global Christian.

2   Be a learner. Decide to go on a learning journey.

»   Set a goal to read or listen to some books on global ministry—a book a month, three this year, etc.

» Listen to some podcasts or digital presentations on missions. Let them stir your heart and challenge your paradigms.

» Want to get serious? Take a Perspectives course. This is a college accredited study available to everyone. It requires high commitment and a fair amount of time and effort but will have a profound and lingering impact on your life. You can find more information at <u>www.perspectives.org</u>. This will teach you about God's heart for a lost world, missiology (the study of effectively ministering in other cultures), and how you and your church can actively engage in the global mission movement.

3 Invest in global work.

» Identify a missionary you can serve from where you are. Build a relationship with them, find out what would help them in their missionary work and do what you can to serve them well. At the same time, I encourage you to ask good and meaningful questions of them. Find out what makes them tick, get a feel for their heart, how they heard God's call on their lives, and more.

» Pray for a missionary and the people they serve. You may even want to gather a handful of others who will commit to praying with you—maybe weekly or monthly, in person or virtually. Pray for their needs and expressed requests, but also pray Scripture over them. Find passages that you want to see realized in the lives of those you are praying for. Keep it real, keep it simple, keep it Spirit-led.

» Invest your finances. Talk is cheap. Jesus said, "Where your treasure is, there will your heart be also," Matthew 6:21. Choose to support a person or ministry that you believe in. Even if it is small or seemingly insignificant, give. You will find yourself becoming a global Christian in the process.

4   Investigate.

In Romans 15:20, the Apostle Paul states, "I make it my ambition to preach the gospel, not where Christ has already been named...." Please notice the intentionality that even Paul needed to exercise in his pursuit of global disciple making. As spiritual as he was, no matter how attuned he was to God's directives, he still needed to "make it his ambition" to participate in bringing the gospel to those in desperate need.

Becoming a global Christian takes intentionality. Isn't this the way God works in all the dimensions of becoming like Jesus? It is never acquired by happenstance, but requires commitment, time, investment and perseverance. But from someone who is still on the journey, every step is worth the effort. God interfaces in this process and makes us rich. At the same time, he accomplishes his redemptive plan through his obedient disciples. Go for it!

"I saw what real faith looked like, recognized my privileged position in the world, understood the depth of darkness among hopeless people and vowed to bring the gospel to those without access to the truths of Jesus Christ."

 My Response

PERSONAL REFLECTION:

Do you think you're ready to become more of a global Christian? Why or why not?

OBSERVATION:

How have you been intentional to engage in missions? How have you lacked intentionality?

Resource suggestions to acquire God's heart for lost people

I've collected a variety resources to help you dive deeper into learning about God's passion for all people. Dive in to one or two of these!

faroffsaints.com/global

ACTION STEP:

What one step could you take to increase your global awareness? (Consider the list in today's reading.)

Help Your Church Succeed

God has a plan for every local church. If you believe that our sovereign God has a plan for your life, you also must believe that God has a plan for your church. Let me go a step further. Because God's ultimate plan is the discipleship of every people group in the world—so much so that he is delaying his return until that is completed—I'm convinced he has a plan for your church to participate in that fulfillment. What does God have for your church to do?

The letter to the Ephesians is written to the church in Ephesus. It is a personal letter to a congregation, not an individual. Ephesians 2:10 states, "For we are his workmanship, created in Christ Jesus for good works, which God prepared beforehand, that we should walk in them." This gives us a compelling reason to believe that if God had a plan for the Ephesian Church, he has a plan for each church today, yours included. He expects each church to carry out the good things he has planned for it to do.

So how do we know what God has planned for our church? First and foremost, he has already spoken clearly through his Word. We certainly need to listen closely. Having been a pastor of local churches for 28 years, I know how easy it is to embrace the things that are encouraging in God's word, to hear those things that affirm us and make us feel good, to highlight those passages of Scripture that align with our plans and agendas for the church. I also know how we can overlook those statements that will require change or confession or sacrifice or a fresh start. Yet, this is what it means to walk in obedience to Christ. It is never easy as an individual believer. It is even more difficult as a church. To walk in obedience as a church takes tremendous courage, an unrelenting resolve to do nothing less and a humility that puts Christ into the true leadership role of your church. When this happens, your pastor is more respected than ever, especially by the Lord. And that's always the best place to be!

Secondly, God most likely has a specific plan that you need to pursue, including your engagement in missions. This takes discernment, prayer and maybe a little assistance to discover well. God has given you the pastor you have for a reason. He has given your church the personality it has to accomplish his plan. He has filled your church with members and attenders with giftings, experiences, passions and abilities that no other church in the whole world has. When you put all these pieces together and then learn to listen well to Lord's whispers, you may very likely find God's specific plan for your church's global ministry.

TRANSACTIONAL VERSUS TRANSFORMATIONAL ENGAGEMENT

A transactional orientation to missions is usually writing a check. This is not bad. I hope more of you will be transactional toward missions. Transactional engagements are needed but it is the beginning of engagement, not the pinnacle of it.

Consider Ellen Livingood's Church Missions Continuum on the next page. Take two minutes to study it and take it in.

God would like to see you and your church move down on this continuum. The 29% of the world's population without access to the gospel is depending on many churches becoming transformationally engaged. As you participate more fully in God's global agenda, you and your church will be transformed. Your hearts will be changed, your priorities adjusted, your generosity increased and your love for Jesus strengthened.

SUPPORTING
Own the program
Perform a duty

SENDING
Own the missionary
Provide a basecamp

PARTNERING
Own the mission
Passionately engage

1 Write a regular support check

2 Launch occasional short term teams and projects

3 Recruit and screen prospective workers

4 Guide & prepare candidates

5 Resource workers

6 Provide 360° care

7 Give attention to accountability & oversight

8 Embrace ministry goals

9 Live into the story

10 Engage multiple ways to reach the goal

11 Find/Mobilize more partners

This is the kind of transformation God desires for every congregation. It does take tremendous courage, however, to begin the journey from transactional to transformational engagement in missions. When your church does this, everybody wins! The pastor, church members, lost people in your community, and those in the world who have never heard of Jesus. Something miraculous happens--truly miraculous because God does something in and through us as a church that only he can do. It's beautiful!

Consider a few more ways you can help your church succeed:

> » **Be a cheerleader, not a Negite.** Remember the people lists in the Old Testament—the Canaanites, Amorites, Hittites, Perizzites, Hivites, and Jebusites? Well, one not mentioned in the Bible, but a dread to every pastor is the Negite. This is the negative-oriented person who rarely says anything positive, but is usually pounding their agenda, criticizing the pastor's way and generally causing a big stink in the church whenever they are there. And a lot of them are trying to influence missions! Don't be a Negite! Instead, be your pastor and staff's best cheerleader. Nothing spiritual has ever been accomplished through negativity anyway. Better than being a Negite is being a learner. If you're confused about what's happening in your church, have an honest conversation with the appropriate pastoral staff. Don't seek to insert your agenda but seek to understand how your church is listening to God and following well. Go ahead and ask honest questions you would like answered, but then cheer them on! I know how difficult it is to lead a congregation. True cheerleaders are like gold to a pastor. They are rare and truly treasured when they play their role well.

> » **Help highlight the role of missionary.** A modern fallacy is that everyone be considered a missionary. I understand the intent, but it is actually counter-productive to missions. Yes, we should all be on mission, but the term missionary is the modern term for the gift of an apostle. Ephesians 4:11-12 states that to the church God "gave the apostles, the prophets, the evangelists, the shepherds and teachers, to equip the saints for the work of ministry, for building up the body of Christ." These five-fold giftings are still given to the church. The unique role of apostle equips someone to be a catalyst for new things, go into places where the gospel isn't to establish new churches and leaders and then go do it again and again. Picture the apostle Paul for

instance and all he did in his missionary work. He was a hand-picked apostle of Jesus Christ (Galatians 2:8). We are all to be witnesses, but a missionary has a specific cross-cultural gifting given to a few that enables them to go places and do things that they are uniquely wired to do. To casually believe we're all missionaries devalues that uniqueness and the high calling of this biblical role of apostle. One quick word of wisdom: Don't make this your soapbox issue, but also be honest about addressing this as the occasions properly arise.

» **Serve on the Outreach or Missions team.** Be a biblical voice for God's agenda. Then help your church find and carry out its role well. You may be gifted to help in strategizing or providing care for missionaries or leading a team that provides care or managing communications with global workers or helping celebrate accomplishments by supported missionaries or being a prayer leader or prayer warrior or being an advocate for your pastoral staff in relation to missions. The opportunities are endless. Understand your passion and giftings and see if you can serve in a way where beautiful blessings will flow.

» **Be a spy.** That's right! Every church needs several spies—those who clearly understand what it takes to be a missionary and watches for candidates to emerge. This can be so fun and incredibly rewarding! I will share more about this on the last day of the journal reading.

There are so many more ways you can help your church succeed in its global engagement. Ask God to help you be a person of godly influence, not someone driven by human effort or a self-made agenda. This makes all the difference. When God is in it, God will use you in stunning ways. You just watch and see.

 My Response

PERSONAL REFLECTION:

What stands out to you most in the reading today and why?

OBSERVATION:

What is the most likely way you can help your church succeed in missions?

Resource suggestions to acquire God's heart for lost people

I've collected a variety resources to help you dive deeper into learning about God's passion for all people. Dive in to one or two of these!

faroffsaints.com/success

ACTION STEP:

Write a short prayer for your church related to global ministry and what you would like your part to be.

Sacrifice and Send

Imagine the tremendous loss by all of Christendom if Saul (Paul) and Barnabas had never been sent by the young vibrant church of Antioch. Their sacrifice impacted all human history. Could God have accomplished his plan another way? Of course. Could Paul and Barnabas have gone without being sent? Yes—but with a model of ministry that would have been far inferior. Could God have used others instead of Paul and Barnabas. Certainly, because God can do anything. But God's stated and best plan for global discipleship is for the local church to send the right people into places that desperately need the gospel.

Let's take a closer look at the Antioch church Acts 13:1-3:

Now there were in the church at Antioch prophets and teachers, Barnabas, Simeon who was called Niger, Lucius of Cyrene, Manaen a lifelong friend of Herod the tetrarch, and Saul. While they were worshiping the Lord and fasting, the Holy Spirit said, "Set apart for me Barnabas and Saul for the work to which I have called them." Then after fasting and praying they laid their hands on them and sent them off.

These three verses contain a lot of valuable information. The short list of gifted people here reflects what we read a bit earlier about the church in Antioch. In Acts 12, we see a young church that is flourishing, largely because they were open to the new things God was doing among them. One of the most significant is that they "spoke to the Hellenists (Greek speaking non-Jews) also, preaching the Lord Jesus. And the hand of the Lord was with them, and a great number who believed turned to the Lord," Acts 12:20b-21. This church was breaking new ground, taking risks, leaning into the Holy Spirit's fresh direction, dedicated to helping disciples grow deep and strong. The two primary teachers—the movers and shakers—were Barnabas and Saul. In large part, this church's raving success was a result of its profoundly gifted and deeply committed leaders.

Think of having Barnabas and Saul in your church. They were godly, knew how to walk by the Spirit, had the gifts of teaching, leading, admonition and encouragement. They were straight talkers who could speak a hard word of truth in a way that helped more than offended. These men had a unique ability to understand the Scriptures of the Old Testament and how they foreshadowed and prepared things for this unique time in history. Wisdom oozed out their words and their insights continued to transform this church into something rare and special.

And then we read that, in response to the Holy Spirit's prompting, they sent them away! How could they do that?

> » They didn't see this as a loss, but an opportunity to expand their influence for the Kingdom of God.

> » They chose to send their best because they knew the lost world needed those kinds of leaders.

> » They chose to release who they had to provide for those without.

Our greatest act of generosity often isn't financial. Giving away gifted people to grow the Kingdom is a stunning and godly act of sending. This is also what God expects of our churches. Whether it's sending people here, near or far, there is greater blessing in sending than in keeping. The upside-down kingdom principles almost always go against our human wisdom and logic. It doesn't make sense to send your best unless God is in it. When he is, you cannot lose by obeying his promptings.

How did the church in Antioch know God's leading in this?

>> They were a worshiping church.

>> They were deep in the Word.

>> They were a praying and fasting church.

>> They were keenly attentive to the Holy Spirit's whispers.

The pastor in me wants to preach a series on each of these characteristics which eventually made them a global force for the Kingdom of God. There is substance and depth to each of the four characteristics listed. They are worth pondering, praying through, engaging in bold assessment and taking the necessary action to be more like the church in Antioch. But here's the bottom line: Because they were spiritually vibrant, they were selfless, purposeful, sacrificial, bold and obedient. Being a sending church is not simply a decision to send. It must be a highly esteemed value that permeates the culture of your congregation. The mission of God for the world must be the driver that leads you to have a vibrant church. If your church is intent on growing for the sake of growth, community respect, or meeting budgets, your vision is way too small. If you are developing a vibrant church to increase your influence hear, near and far, then go for it! And be selfless in the process. That's the Kingdom way.

Jesus highly valued sending. In fact, there is a good argument to believe that the church is not the church God intends unless it is a sending church. When Jesus rose from the grave and saw his disciples again for the first time, the first statement after settling them down from their fright was simply this: "As the Father has sent me, so I am sending you," John 20:21. Consider a few quick observations on this text:

>> The Greek word for "as" is Kathos, a term of comparison. When Jesus tells them this, they are compelled to think about how the Father has sent Jesus, because this is the way Jesus is now sending them.

>> The Father's sending of Jesus was very intentional. It was not serendipitous—something that just happened. There was much thought and planning that went into this endeavor.

>> The Father sent Jesus to raise up senders, not just send. Jesus' mission would have been short-lived and severely limited in scope if He did not incorporate multiplication as his primary strategy.

>> The Father sent Jesus to be selfless, suffer, and be long-term focused. This may go against what our current Christian culture values or measures as success.

Even in this cursory look at sending, I hope you see that this is central to the mission of God in our world. It is to be a church's spiritual endeavor that requires commitment, intentionality and the Holy Spirit's leadership.

SACRIFICE

I'm humbled by what missionaries sacrifice to go serve in the world. Each one sacrifices in different ways depending on their life situations and cross-cultural realities. Consider a few sacrifices that virtually every missionary makes when they choose to go:

>> The familiar for the unfamiliar.

>> They leave family behind, including aging parents and college bound children.

>> Separation from friends and social circles they've developed for a lifetime.

>> Peace for stress.

» The comforts of home.

» A language they can easily speak to become like little children in their verbal skills.

» The material luxuries of America.

» A home church.

» An easily accessible education system for their children.

» A career that could be culturally valued and financially lucrative.

There are many more sacrifices that global workers make. These sacrifices affect them every single day. For missionaries, sacrifice and difficulty are largely a way of life. This is not an exaggeration in the least.

How about you? Are you sacrificing to help them go? Or do you feel that the primary sacrifice for global discipleship is on the shoulders of those called to go? If not, what does sacrifice look like for those who send?

I've always been inspired by King David's statement on Araunah's threshing floor in 1 Chronicles 21. A plague was ravaging Israel and David knew it was his fault. Only he could stop the plague by offering a sacrifice to the Lord. Being near the threshing floor of a farmer named Araunah, David asked for what was needed to make this urgent sacrifice to the Lord. Araunah kindly offered to give David everything he needed, but David would not take it without paying a price: "I will not present burnt offerings that have cost me nothing," I Chronicles 21:24b. God responds to sacrifice. Giving out of our abundance is good and is to be expected, but where does sacrifice come in? What could you give up to send missionaries to the least-reached of the world? What lifestyle change could you make that will honor the Lord in your giving? Are you willing to sacrifice along with those who are sent?

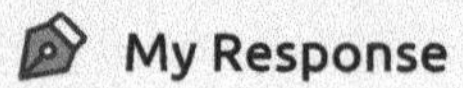 My Response

PERSONAL REFLECTION:

Jot down a few thoughts about the Antioch church that stand out to you.

OBSERVATION:

What would it take for your church to become a more significant sending church?

Resource suggestions to acquire God's heart for lost people

I've collected a variety resources to help you dive deeper into learning about God's passion for all people. Dive in to one or two of these!

faroffsaints.com/sacrifice

ACTION STEP:

What thoughts do you have about sacrificing to send? Talk to God about this and listen for what He says to you.

Go! Plant Seeds, Too

When Jesus began his disciple-making ministry on the shores of Galilee, each potential disciple needed to make a decision. Will I follow? That meant a lot of things, like leaving their work, family, home, everyday routines and the comfortable social circles they had nurtured. Maybe as much as anything, they needed to leave their dreams.

Jim and Ina had dreams of what they would do when they reached retirement. Jim especially. He was a medical doctor his entire career. He dreamed of finally being done with the demanding lifestyle of a doctor and instead looked forward to working in his garden, fishing and catching up on his reading. He couldn't wait!

Jim and Ina were also deeply committed believers. At Jim's age of 62, as their retirement season approached, they assessed the situation and decided they would go serve on the mission field for two years. After that, they could pick up their dream and live THE life!

There was a fledgling health clinic in a hardship post in Banyo, Cameroon that could use their skills. It was remote, far removed from what we would consider civilization and surrounded by Muslims, most of whom had never heard of Jesus. With Holy Spirit courage and a resolve to do their part, they headed to Africa.

I met Jim and Ina for the first time in the eleventh year of their missionary service. I flew by helicopter to meet them—it would have taken 12 hours by car to reach Banyo. What I found was no longer a fledgling clinic, but a full-fledged hospital. When I arrived, crowds of people were in the waiting area outside, all glued to The Jesus Film in the Fulfulde language being played on a large-screen TV. For many, this was the first time they had ever heard the story of Jesus. As for the hospital, they were in the process of adding a new maternity wing. Too many moms had been dying in childbirth. I met two Cameroonian surgeons who had been trained by our missionaries. All the staff were Africans, including two converted Muslims who now started and operated the only radio station in the area. This was a daily source of practical information for people providing everything from news to weather reports to social events. They also wove the gospel into their broadcasts throughout the day. This was transformational ministry, all because a couple decided to give "two" years of service to the suffering and lost in Cameroon.

A couple days later, as I was climbing a mountain with 73-year-old Jim, I asked him, "How long do you plan to keep doing this?" Without a moment of hesitation, he stated, "Ten to twelve more years as the Lord gives me strength!" He then went on to say, "When I think back of what I wanted to do when I retired—when I reflect on the dreams I had for my life—I'm so grateful God led me to this place. There's nothing I would rather do in my retirement than this!"

When we choose to go, there will be things we need to give up. Yet God is waiting to give you something better, richer, more fulfilling and more eternally significant than we can imagine.

What does it take to be a missionary? Let me give you my best short list:

1   **A readiness to go.** Jesus boldly stated that nothing should come before him if you intend to be his disciple, "If anyone comes to me and does not hate his own father and mother and wife and children and brothers and sisters, yes and even his own life, he cannot be my disciple," Luke 14:26. Using hyperbole by using the word "hate",

Jesus is emphasizing his ultimate place and price he expects of his disciples. Missionaries live this in ways few others do. Literally, they leave those who are most dear to them to go live among people they have never met. There is a tremendous price that global workers pay, but they do it with joy, purpose and an anticipation that God is going to use their sacrifice to make disciples where they are desperately needed.

2 **An apostolic gifting.** "Apostle" in the Bible refers to Jesus' twelve disciples, but it encompasses much more. The gift of apostleship is critical to the Kingdom of God expanding to new places and unreached people. "Apostle" literally means a delegate, messenger or one that is sent. These are people that go to places where few people go to represent Christ. This gifting encompasses the characteristics of courage, faith, strength, resilience, being a learner, being adaptable, living with humbleness and being driven for those who still need Jesus. Of all the apostles in the Bible, we know the most about Paul. Look at him and you get a snapshot of one of the best. They are rare and wonderful people whom God wants to use in unique ways in least-reached regions to see his Kingdom come and his will be done.

3 **A calling.** Luke was definitely called, but in a support role. Not all who are called are apostles. Luke was a missionary, but did not have the same gifting as Paul. He was there to serve Paul, the team members and those who needed to embrace the gospel of Jesus Christ. He risked much, sacrificed tremendously, served diligently and represented Jesus well. He was also a pretty good writer. Luke could have only done this because this was God's plan for his life. He was called by God, set apart for this work of bringing the gospel to new regions of the world.

Knowing if you're called is tricky. I have seen wonderful people with very good intentions who have been convinced that God is calling them to be a missionary. It was obvious to everyone else that this was not the case. So how do we know if we're called?

>> First, if you're not doing it here, you won't be doing it there. Check your track record. Are you making disciples here? What you may feel God is calling you to do in another place must be your passion here. Is there fruit?

>> Second, let others tell you. Even Barnabas and Saul had others tell them that they were to go. The Lord told the church leaders and the leaders spoke into Barnabas and Saul's lives. It's OK to ask your pastor and church leaders, too. But ask them to be totally honest about what they see in you.

>> Third, seek wisdom from those already sent. God has given great wisdom to those working in the world of missions. They will help you assess yourself, find your strengths and weaknesses, tell you if you're ready or called or not called. Trust them to be a voice that God uses in your life as you seek his will. (If you're interested in being assessed, write us at missions@converge.org)

4 **Personal health.** A missionary must be physically, spiritually, relationally and emotionally healthy. None of us are perfect in any of these areas, but the demands of living cross-culturally, often in undeveloped areas, puts each of these dimensions to the test. Average marriages will not survive the mission field. The daily stresses of life along with the spiritual warfare you will experience will test the resolve of your commitment and happiness together. If any of these health categories is an issue, maybe you can change that. Begin a process of developing health in the area that is keeping you from going. If the health issues cannot be resolved (and sometimes it cannot), consider being a standout sender. There's nothing wrong with that!

It would be wrong to go through these four weeks without you considering the possibility of going. It's rarely too late to begin your missionary service—nor too early. I challenge you to ask God to speak to you and lead you in the way he wants you to go. Pray in the spirit of the Psalmist when he said, "Let me hear of your unfailing love each morning, for I am trusting you. Show me where to walk, for I give myself to you," Psalm 143:8.

GOING WHILE STAYING

When Jesus healed the wildly demonized man in the region of the Decapolis, "the man begged to go with him. But Jesus said, 'No, go home to your family, and tell them everything the Lord has done for you and how merciful he has been,'" Mark 5:18b-19.

Sometimes Jesus wants us to stay where we are.

One of the unique things happening in these days is the massive diaspora—the scattering of people from around the world to every place in the world. Many of those people have moved into our neighborhoods, schools, and workplaces. And many of these people are from people groups that have had little or no exposure to Jesus.

To present the gospel effectively to many of these people is as radical a cross-cultural challenge as any missionary faces in their contexts. It takes intentionality, courage, preparation, Holy Spirit leading, much prayer, patience, and a long-term commitment. It takes going across the street to make a connection or inviting them into your home for a risky adventure or stepping into their world to prove your respect for them. I'm convinced that this is often where our greatest spiritual development takes place. Step out of the familiar into the terrain of faith and courageous obedience just because somebody needs to eventually know about Jesus. Don't rush it, though. It's usually a long obedience in the right direction.

It's very probable that the immigrants and others in your sphere of influence are there because God put them there so you can be Jesus to them. Take the challenge—"go" while staying where you are.

HOW TO SPOT A MISSIONARY

Want a great ministry? Plant seeds into the lives of potential missionaries. I'm convinced that this is one of the most influential ministry practices most overlooked. And it's so simple! And it's really fun!

Dan and Tina were in our congregation in Minnesota. They were also friends for most of my life.

There was a need in Africa for a strong leader, organizer, someone with business acumen and a risk-taker to replace retiring missionaries leading an outstanding ministry there. I saw Dan as having all the characteristics needed to lead this ministry. Dan was also one of those people our church felt was indispensable. He could (and did) do just about anything and everything. If there was a need, a problem or new project—call Dan. His capabilities and service quotient was off the charts.

Tina was on my church staff leading Early Childhood ministries. Having come to know Jesus in an almost miraculous way at age four, she was driven to have a ministry to young children, not just provide childcare. And she was amazing. She also became one of our best recruiters and leaders of volunteers. At the time that this story took place, Tina had 110 volunteers in her ministry department. By the way, the ministry in Africa I suspected was for them was 80% about children—caring for them, giving them homes, new parents, loving on them, sharing Jesus, etc.

I met Dan for a casual lunch one day. In the midst of some nice conversation, I dropped a seed. "Dan, I think you and Tina should consider going to Africa to take over the ministry there." Dan looked at me aghast, "Why in the world would I do that?" Without getting into the rest of the conversation, let me just say the thought had never entered his or Tina's mind. After telling Dan why I thought they would be a good fit and encouraging them to think and pray about it, we parted ways. The seed was planted.

Six months later, Dan and Tina visited the ministry in Africa for the first time to see if God would tell them anything. He did—and they went. For many years, they led that ministry with skill, ingenuity, joy and great results. But Dan and Tina would have never gone if a seed had not been planted.

Do you see the power of planting the seeds of missionary service in others? We may see something in someone, but we rarely tell them. It has been stated that between 1% and 4% of any congregation has the unique gift mix of a missionary. Do the math—you have missionary candidates in your church. The power of a word spoken can be life-changing for these people.

Would you consider making this your ministry? Would you ask God to give you the eyes of Jesus to see those who might be sent? It's not necessary to always be right in your assessment. Just plant seeds. A seed never planted will never grow.

Jesus said, "Pray to the Lord of the Harvest that he would send workers into his harvest." You can be a significant part in seeing the Lord's desire fulfilled in our lifetimes. Go plant those seeds!

My Response

PERSONAL REFLECTION:

Do you think God may be calling you into missionary service? Why or why not?

OBSERVATION:

Write down the names of two or three people you think may be potential missionaries. And then plan a simple way to plant that seed into their lives.

Resource suggestions to acquire God's heart for lost people

I've collected a variety resources to help you dive deeper into learning about God's passion for all people. Dive in to one or two of these!

faroffsaints.com/seeds

ACTION STEP:

Then jot down one or two things that may be next steps for you in becoming more of a global Christian.

WEEK FOUR TAKE AWAY:

Of all you read and experienced in Far Off Saints this week, what one truth will you embrace or action you will take?

SMALL GROUP MATERIALS

How Can I Not Be Far Off?

GETTING STARTED: (5 MINUTES)

Spend a little time mingling and catching up with your Far Off Saints group members.

Begin with Prayer, dedicating this week of Far Off Saints to the Lord. Ask him to help you finish your journal well and meet you powerfully as you engage in his Word and with one another today.

BREAKING THE ICE: (10 MINUTES)

From our Far Off Saints readings so far in week four, what has captured your attention or challenged you significantly? Explain if possible.

VIDEO TEACHING: (30 MINUTES)

» Watch #4 – <u>Washing Jesus' Feet</u>

» What spoke to you most from today's teaching?

» Did God whisper anything to you when asked to wash Jesus' feet?

» Follow up Question: Does anyone have a story when you did wash Jesus' feet and what that did to you? And don't

worry about talking about yourself. We want to learn from one another's experiences.

SCRIPTURE STUDY: 1CORINTHIANS 9:19-27 (30 MINUTES)

Read 1 Corinthians 9:19-23

>> What does Paul mean in verse 19?

>> How do you think Paul adapted to...

>> Become as a Jew to win Jews?

>> Become as one under the law?

>> Become as one outside the law?

>> Become weak?

>> How would you state verses 22b-23 in your own words?

>> What does this tell you about Paul?

>> What does this tell you about the value of the gospel for lost people?

Read 1 Corinthians 9:24-27.

>> What immediately stands out to you as you hear this Scripture?

>> Keeping our previous verses in mind, how does this inform us about carrying out our God-given ministry roles?

>> What disciplines are needed to succeed in your calling as Jesus' disciple?

>> How does this passage as a whole challenge you to better serve the lost here, near and far off?

CONCLUSION: (15 MINUTES)

» What is your take-away from this evening? (That is, what is your next step with what you've heard and experienced?)

» Break into groups of two or three for prayer. Pray for one another specifically about what God has speaking to them through this study.

» Leader, close in prayer for all. Especially ask God to do a new thing in people's lives and in your church as this study comes to a conclusion.

One More Thing

Thank you for engaging with Far Off Saints. I hope the daring dive into the Scriptures, the fresh observations from the world, and the telling insights about the task before us has stimulated your mind and stirred your heart.

Let me challenge you with one last thing. It is too easy to live our spiritual lives only in our heads and emotions. We can cheerfully sit in a Sunday morning church service, agree with a powerfully biblical sermon, sings songs that applaud God's character and affirm our mission. We might feel spiritually uplifted. And that's good! But we can also erroneously think feeling good about God's word and experiencing a flood of emotions in worship is what it's all about. We can become consumers who treat God's word like salve on a sore or a feast to a hearty appetite. It's the trap of thinking God is here to stimulate and soothe us more than challenge and mobilize us.

An honest reading of God's Word makes it uncompromisingly clear that we are called to a daring mission when we become God's children. It is not about us! It is about God's agenda and God's glory!

Consider a few verses from Hebrews 11:

It would take too long to recount the stories of the faith of Gideon, Barak, Samson, Jephthah, David, Samuel, and all the prophets. By faith these people overthrew kingdoms, ruled with justice, and received what God had promised them. They shut the mouths of lions, quenched the flames of fire, and escaped death by the edge of the sword. Their weakness was turned to strength. They became strong in battle and put whole armies to flight. Women received their loved ones back again from death.

But others were tortured, refusing to turn from God in order to be set free. They placed their hope in a better life after the resurrection. Some were jeered at, and their backs were cut open with whips. Others were chained in prisons. Some died by stoning, some were sawed in half, and others were killed with the sword. Some went about wearing skins of sheep and goats, destitute and oppressed and mistreated. They were too good for this world, wandering over deserts and mountains, hiding in caves and holes in the ground. (verses 32-38, NLT)

For me, these verses sting a bit. I really like to be comfortable. I cherish my middle-class American lifestyle where I can manage my time, commitments and relationships. In contrast, I'm not too thrilled to have someone else—even God—impose their expectations on me. I've realized that being in control is one of the gods in my life I need to relinquish. It's easy to sing, "I surrender all," but it's quite another thing to do it! Especially when many who have gone before us have suffered horribly because they followed God's plan!

Before you walk away from Far Off Saints, I ask that you wrestle with how you will obey what God has whispered to you, come what may. It may be a simple next step. It could be a radical life change. Could it be a sacrifice you should make? Maybe God is telling you to pray and consider for a season what he has for you in his Great Commission. But for sure, don't walk away without deciding what next step you will take in relation to this great task of taking the gospel to those who still need to hear of Jesus.

Let me end where we began in this study. When the Holy Spirit interrupted Pentecost like a tsunami on the diverse crowd of thousands, a previously tepid Peter courageously stood and boldly delivered the first ever message for Christ's church. The gospel of Jesus was clearly explained. The convicted crowd begged for direction on what they should do next. Peter then instructed the crowd to repent for inner transformation and be baptized for public proclamation. Don't miss this now—Peter's next statement is about the critical role of Jesus' disciples. He declared, "this promise is for you, your children and for all who are far off."

May God guide you beautifully into what he has next for you. Step into it with courage!

For God's glory and all who are far off,

Ivan Veldhuizen

It Takes A Team!

It takes a very good team to produce a project like this. There are many people that have invested themselves into Far Off Saints long before it was a sure thing. A few that stand out are:

My wife Susan, thanks for your undying support and consistent encouragement to keep at it. You're an outstanding editor, too! This would never have been completed without you.

The Arrival Creative team, Shane Veldhuizen and Joseph Boyle, you guys rock! You took my simple ideas and inserted creativity and excellence into the entire package.

My Executive Assistant, Kim Skundrich, you made sure I always set time aside to keep this project moving forward.

Kevin McGhee, my friend and colleague in ministry, you picked up so many of my responsibilities so I could finish this important work.

Gloria Lopez who hosted the teaching videos like a star, but also helped get the word out about Far Off Saints with her wonderful communications team at Converge.

"The Crowd"—all of you who came to the teaching shoot-day not having a clue what you were getting into. Thanks for taking the risk. A special shout out to Luke Heinsch who kept us looking to Jesus that day!

Our groupie friends who prayed this into reality. I do believe God answered those prayers to provide this tool he will use for his glory. Thank you!

The Five Great Commissions In Review

Jesus left us with a task. After all Jesus did, taught, suffered and overcame, he brought clarity to his disciples about what was to happen after his departure. These teachings are not equal in weight with all other passages of Scripture. These passages frame our understanding of most of the letters of the New Testament. These words of Jesus point us in a direction, both in what we are to accomplish as his followers and how we are to get that done.

Prayerfully allow these five records of The Great Commission to wash over your mind and heart. Maybe you've never seen them all together before. Allow the weight and significance of these directives realign your orientation and adjust your course to walk in step with what Jesus is calling his church to do.

Here are the five statements of Jesus with brief bullet point observations:

And Jesus came and said to them, "All authority in heaven and on earth has been given to me. [19] Go therefore and make disciples of all nations, baptizing them in the name of the Father and of the Son and of the Holy Spirit, [20] teaching them to observe all that I have commanded you. And behold, I am with you always, to the end of the age." Matthew 28:18-20

» Jesus forwards his authority over all things to his followers.

» The primary task is to disciple the nations (ethnic groups of the world).

» We are to be intentionally thorough as we pour Truth into new disciples for obedience.

And he said to them, "Go into all the world and proclaim the gospel to the whole creation. ¹⁶ Whoever believes and is baptized will be saved, but whoever does not believe will be condemned. ¹⁷ And these signs will accompany those who believe: in my name they will cast out demons; they will speak in new tongues; ¹⁸ they will pick up serpents with their hands; and if they drink any deadly poison, it will not hurt them; they will lay their hands on the sick, and they will recover." Mark 16:15-18

» The primary task is to proclaim the truth of Jesus to the entire world.

» This task will either bring life or death to those who hear.

» The work would be accompanied by obvious signs and miracles testifying to the power of God and the truth of this message.

Then he opened their minds to understand the Scriptures, ⁴⁶ and said to them, "Thus it is written, that the Christ should suffer and on the third day rise from the dead, ⁴⁷ and that repentance for the forgiveness of sins should be proclaimed in his name to all nations, beginning from Jerusalem. ⁴⁸ You are witnesses of these things. ⁴⁹ And behold, I am sending the promise of my Father upon you. But stay in the city until you are clothed with power from on high." Luke 24:45-49

» Understanding the truth of the Scriptures is essential for success in the mission.

» The primary task is to proclaim forgiveness of sins to all nations, beginning where they were.

» We are to never attempt this great task without the Holy Spirit as our promised gift from the Father.

Jesus said to them again, "Peace be with you. As the Father has sent me, even so I am sending you." [22] *And when he had said this, he breathed on them and said to them, "Receive the Holy Spirit.* [23] *If you forgive the sins of any, they are forgiven them; if you withhold forgiveness from any, it is withheld." John 20:21-23*

» Jesus first words to his disciples after the resurrection emphasized the critical role of sending others into the world.

» The Holy Spirit is either given or will be given and Jesus' followers are to receive him.

» Great authority is entrusted to Jesus' disciples—to forgive or not forgive sins.

"But you will receive power when the Holy Spirit has come upon you, and you will be my witnesses in Jerusalem and in all Judea and Samaria, and to the end of the earth." Acts 1:8

» Jesus' followers need the Holy Spirit to do what He is telling us to do.

» We are to be his witnesses here, near and far, even to the least and last on planet earth.

Can you comprehend how this can be? Two thousand years ago, Jesus told us to disciple all the ethne' (ethnic groups) of the world and we still haven't accomplished the task. Those far off saints live with the greatest injustice in the world. 29% of the world's population has no access to the gospel. Certainly, there are lots of questions we could have about what that means:

1   If people heard the gospel once and since have forsaken it, does that count in God's economy? For instance, the Apostle Paul worked so

hard in Asia Minor, specifically Macedonia and Greece. Today, there is tiny fraction of biblical believers in these parts. Have they had their chance? Do we not focus here? Or does this still fall into God's "lost sheep" orientation?

2   What does "reached" mean? In the missions world, we have categorized our work so we can easily understand one another when we talk about the needs of the world. In Converge, we refer to "least-reached" as 4% or less evangelical. Missiologists have categorized "unreached" as an ethnolinguistic group that is 2% or less evangelical, without the capacity to reach the rest of their people without outside intervention. "Unengaged unreached people groups" are those with no known believers, no churches and no-one currently working among them to establish Christ's church. It's helpful to have these terms, but we don't presume to put parameters on God's way of evaluating things. How does God see it? When has a people group had ample opportunity to embrace Jesus so they are considered evangelized?

3   Is evangelism enough, or must we see multiplicative discipleship take place for us to comply with the "make disciples" directive?

There are different ways of counting the people groups in the world. For instance, are all Japanese one unreached people group (120 million), or are there quite a number—those in south America, North America, Europe, and wherever communities of Japanese have settled? See how complicated missions can be?

Has the church failed in her task, or is God carefully carrying out His ultimate plan? At the risk of sounding simplistic, I would say both.

1   The church has languished in its task of global discipleship

It doesn't help to point out blame if we don't reflect enough to change course in our day and time. My intent is not to point the finger at those who have gone before. My hope is that, with a little reflection, we can identify some errors and make course corrections so we can do better.

2   God is carefully carrying out His ultimate plan.

As we think of the many people groups still unreached with the gospel, it is also important for us to understand the unfolding of recent history. We actually didn't understand how God saw the society of humans very well until the 1970s. Remember Ralph Winter? This was the first time there was a full embrace of both technology (to manage the data) and new understanding plied together in such a way that it gave traction to the biblical intentions of God. God always understood what made people groups, but we didn't. God knew from the Tower of Babel how language would separate peoples from one another. God knew the unique challenges of culture and the impenetrable walls that man-made religions would bring. God always knew that mountains and islands and rivers and glaciers and forests and cities and wars and family hostilities would divide the world into 17,000 different identifiable people groups. We didn't get it, but God did.